MY

BROTHER,

THE

RIVER

CHARLES LYTTON

Book design by PenworthyLLC

Line art by Patsy Faires

Cover photo by John Kline,

John's Camera Corner and Gentry Studio

Blacksburg, Virginia

ISBN: 0-9852732-4-0

EAN-13: 978-0-9852732-4-8

No man ever steps
in the same river twice,
for it's not the same river
and he's not the same man
  Heraclitus

CONTENTS

This book is dedicated to Mr. Kevan Harris. He is a cousin of mine, but more than that he is a true friend. He is a role model for being a good husband and the father of two wonderful sons. He can build about anything. Yes, he shares with me some of that magnificent Lytton/Dehart blood and gene pool. I am aware of no better cross-breeding. He's a fine cook, too. He can smoke a mean set of baby-back ribs and pork loins. Sometimes I think that he ort to be on one of those afternoon cooking shows.

Grinning from ear to ear, Kevan can labor all day long behind a hay baler with the sweat running down his face and back. Another thing about him: he loves a good long drink of XXX moonshine that comes from an old white oak keg! That in itself proves there is a blood link between us. "Like father and like grandfather," so they say. Or as they say on River Ridge, "A round apple will roll down the hill until it hits something." The more modern reader needs to hear something like this. We do just what we were taught as children. We drink a lot, eat a lot and some say we talk far too much.

Some Things Are Not So Funny

I will shake the hand of a man who doesn't carry a pocketknife, but I ain't going to hold onto it too long!

Most of the stories I've written have been about something funny or some dumb stuff that I have done. Well, truth is, River Ridge was not without its sad, mean side. I am guessing that I was about 10 or 11 years old at the time of this story. It takes place at Uncle Nelson's hog-scalding platform.

I have spent my day pulling hair off of hogs or helping drag dead hogs from their pen to the scalding barrel and running to hunt and fetch pans and tools. We have just finished the hog-killing, and the last of 8 or 10 hogs is on the pole. For the past few minutes, I have been washing the blood from inside the cavity of the last hog. Right about now, every adult and older cousin is pretty much starting to enjoy a little nip. Elmer (That's my dad, which you already know, if you've read any of the other books.) says for me to stop wasting wash water. Like a fool I do not. I learned early that you just do not play around when men are starting to hit the bottle.

Daddy just gets up and walks over to the pole where all the dead hogs are hanging and grabs the waterhose from my hand. I will never forget what he does next. Rather than pitch the hose down, or yell at me to stop, he rares back and hits me across my back with the garden hose. The spray nozzle is still attached. He almost knocks the breath out of me. I stumble forward a few feet. The group is as quiet as an empty church.

Now I break into a run. I do not want the others to see my chin wiggling and me fight back tears or the giant red welt growing across my bare back. I run for home. A little while later Mod Snider and Gilbert Hilton come looking for me. As they grow near to the house, I hear one of them say, "Pickle has no call to treat that boy like a dog and work the stuffings (They did not say stuffings, but I do not want to hurt your ears.) out of him all the time."

I think the second most hurtful part was Daddy not even coming to check on me. I guess there was still far too much good apple brandy to be drunk up for him to be worrying about children and family. I think that his pride got in his way some, too. He was sorry that he had reacted the way he had, but there was no way he could say it. Truly, Daddy did not mean to hit me. He just lost control for a second.

Mr. Hilton said one time, "Them Lyttons just kind of raised themselves without much knowledge of a father." As for me, I always felt that some days you were worth more or more appreciated, and some days you needed to give Elmer lots of room. He had a way of keeping you in your place, all right. These days I try real hard not to be so much like Daddy in this regard.

Another thing that Elmer liked to do was scream and argue with people before breakfast. Just recently I heard a man tell a story about a man—not Elmer—he once knew. What the feller said was something like: "If I get home and supper is not hot and ready on the table, there will be hell to pay. And if I get home and supper is waiting for me, I will be damned if I eat even one bite."

Elmer truly wasn't that bad, but the guy writing that story may have known my dad. I now think on these mornings what he got into was an outgrowth of having a hangover or a headache.

Most any morning, though, if his eggs were not cooked exactly the way he wanted, someone was going to get a very loud tongue-lashing. Most of the time it was Mom that got the cussing. The funny thing with the eggs was his taste changed each day. Mom had to guess. Elmer was not going to give anyone a hint.

Well anyway, for some reason one morning as Daddy went down the stairs, I saw him take off his hat and pitch it under my bed. When he got to the kitchen, I heard him scream, "Get them all up. I want my hat, and I want it now."

I was now standing behind him with the hat on my head. I said, "Here is your hat." He grabbed the hat off my head and stomped out of the house without eating his breakfast. He did not even so much as take his lunch. Mom warned me right then that, come night, I'd best stay out of the way and real quiet.

Wash Day

Uncle Shorty would say, "Be real careful what you get yourself into. You never know what might happen if-n you get caught."

Wash day at Grandmother's was a hard full day for all the women. I always thought that this was some real rough women's work. Men just seemed like they were always gone. Some were out at public work, some were out on the farm, while others were deep in the earth—they were miners. Me, I wished I could just hide someplace. But often I was too little to run very fast. I was always being caught!

About every two weeks, we washed clothes. The day always started off before breakfast. Every pot, pan and bucket that would hold water was carried outside to the cistern and pumped full of water. Grandmother, Mother and Aunt Maude carried the buckets and pots back into the house and set them on top of the wood cookstove in Grandmother's kitchen.

Even in the winter, the kitchen got hot enough for a fresh egg to boil sitting on the kitchen table in one of Grandmother's green glass bowls. In the cooler months of the year this wasn't so bad, but in the summer months, it was raging hot in the kitchen.

When it got too hot, Grandmother moved heating the wash water outside. A fire was built under one of the big 20-gallon, cast iron kettles to make sure there would be hot water all day long. The dirty, cool gray-looking water was carried to the flowers, but not until it was about as dirty as I was.

Once the water started to heat up, the big old wringer machine was carried out into the yard and set on the concrete sidewalk. If you set it on the ground, the mud would get tracked back into the house. The old washing machine was filled with hot water, soap powder, and as many dirty clothes as you could stuff into it. When the "on" switch was mashed, that thing would go to jumping up and down, churning, moaning and pounding. A second tub was set on a table right behind the wringer and filled with boiling hot water, too.

After awhile, one of the women would say, "Them clothes have done washing by now." The wet clothes were then fed into the wringer. A second person guided the clothes into the big zinc tub of boiling-hot rinse water. More often than not, the rinsed clothes were then fed back through the wringer a second time, just to get more of the water out. This was all done barehanded, too. The wet clothes were carried to the clotheslines in the back yard to dry.

The old wringer looked like if you messed up and got caught, it would drag you into the tub and mash you flat, then spit you out in the rinse water tub. If this happened, you would be no thicker than a piece of Wrigley's spearmint gum.

The ladies' hands were always red and chapped from this job. I ain't going to talk about ironing sheets and pillowcases or the hours spent at the ironing board working on old cotton shirts and pants. I will tell you that Grandmother would wash Uncle Shorty's mining hats. She rinsed them in a little pan of starch water and stretched  them over a one- gallon metal can. When the hats were dry, you could thump them like a watermelon. Grandmother would line them up on the top of the cabinet on the back porch. Uncle Shorty liked to have a clean hat when he headed off to the mines.

I, too, got washed in the rinse water. After the last loads of clothes were on the clothesline, I was caught up and put into the rinse tub. Being washed out in the yard in a big zinc bathtub with the last of the wash water was kind of fun. The water was already a little dirty. Everybody—adults—just laughed and joked, saying they wanted to run me through the wringer, too.

Elmer and Shorty walked by and whispered in my ear, "Now don't stand up too quick and get your peter hung in the wringer. It just might pull it off all the way to the back of your ass! Then you will have a hard time peeing."

Mom would just say, "You pay them no mind; that ain't going to happen."

Elmer Digging at the Old Spring

Change is always coming. Most of the time you never see it or know it until it is upon you.

As a kid, I always disliked being sent to the spring holler to look for the milk cows and the horses. I think the animals knew that this was about as far away from the barn as they could go. I am convinced that they knew that no one was going down over that steep hill after them. Except me, that is. Later I would go to thinking the animals went to the spring holler because of cool spring water and the shade of the big trees. There was always a breeze blowing up the holler off of the river. Horses and cows will drink pond water and get by just fine, but I think that they are like fat little boys in the sense that they, too, like cool, clean spring water that has rolled over three or more rocks. About everybody knows that impure water can be purified by letting it flow over three rocks. Well, that's what the old people would tell me. So, I always had the purest water around, and it tasted good, too.

The old spring was a long ways down over the hill from the Lytton Cemetery, not far from the present-day railroad crossing. There is no way to reach the spring except to walk through hundreds of small cedar trees and millions of blackberry briars and fight through tall honeysuckles growing up every tree. All the while, you're falling over limestone outcroppings. It isn't that far a walk, but it is damn near impossible to get back in there and harder than Chinese arithmetic to get back out. Me, I always followed the old car road and the bottom of the hill to the railroad crossing and fought my way up the big ditch. If I was lucky enough to find the horse, holding on to his or her tail was the easiest way out.

It was a fine spring morning. Warm air was stirring, and the sky was blue as indigo. Warm breezes of spring blew in about every direction. Maple trees already had leaves about the size of a small squirrel's ear. Buds on all the other trees were swelling up with little streaks of red. Some of the locals had already made holes in the maple trees for collecting sap to make maple syrup. The dogwoods and redbuds along the cliffs above the railroad and river would be in flower just any day. Crocuses in Grandmother's and Aunt Tootie's yards were already blooming. "Old people will soon be taking off their long winter underwear," Luther Snider reminded me.

One day, out of the blue, Daddy asked me to find a pick and a long-handled shovel. I asked him what he was going to do. He quietly informed me that he was going to walk through the holler and follow the old car road to the spring. "We are

9

going to clean out the spring and dig a small pond for the milk cows and horses to drink from."

We did this little chore about every six months. In the past few years we had discovered there was less water running from the spring each year. Up the hill above the spring, three houses now stood. All the grownups said that the wells supplying water to these houses had lowered the water table, and there just wasn't the volume of water in the earth that had once been there. But Elmer was not convinced of this. The old spring was not more than 250 feet, in vertical elevation, above the New River and not more than 350 feet below the level of the first house.

Elmer said, "Hell, that water is coming from the river, and we just have to look for it until we find it. That water has been in the spring since I was a little boy. When Mamaw moved to River Ridge, people could stop and water their horses there, too. It was a sight easier to stop and get a drink from the trickle of water from the spring than to walk down to the river."

As we neared the spring, Daddy said, "Look at that big, wide ditch. It must have taken a million years for that little spring to carve that out. There is plenty of water in the old spring."

Thinking back to that day, I now realize there was just a certain amount of wishing in his voice and actions. I don't think it was water Daddy was looking for; it was a fond childhood memory. You know, one full of cool water, big trees filled with squirrels and a place for him to escape from Grandmother.

When we walked up the path, he could remember having to walk up that hill to look for the milk cows and horses the same exact way I was doing now. He could remember the cool taste of the water on hot summer afternoons looking for the milk cows.

We spent the whole day digging in the spring. Daddy also spent the whole day telling stories of funny things he had done in this little valley. It must have been a gathering place for the boys and girls on their way to the river.

We raked out all of the old leaves and sticks and removed all of the rocks that had fallen into the spring since the last time we cleaned it. We dug out a small collection pond at the edge of the big ditch. Then we dug a hole deep back into the mountain. We found that the deeper we dug, the more water flowed. But, there was still almost no water.

As the day went on, Gilbert Hilton, Mod Snider and Sam Smith all joined us. They lived on top of the hill. Each had well water, and everyone speculated that their well was drilled into the same ungrounded reservoir of underground water. Their only question was, "Having any luck?" Someone remarked: "Not much water any more, is it? The old spring is going dry. It just ain't got no more water in it."

After awhile, we all got tired and went back to the house. On Sunday morning Daddy and I walked back to the spring. We found a small deep pool of the coolest, best-tasting water anyone ever drank. There were birds and animal tracks around the pool. Elmer was as happy as any person you ever saw!

When I was a kid, I was in and out of the holler on pretty regular basis. There were some real good trees over there for climbing. I guess I, too, kept an eye on the old spring. When the days got hot and trees completely leafed out, the spring just vanished. Every day trees drink lots of water. These trees drank the spring dry. "It is so dry that even the crawfish and spring lizards are gone." Daddy was taken aback by this. "That damn water is over there!"

Well, there was a man down in McCoy who had a backhoe. Daddy hired him to come over and clean out the spring. Mr. Smith drove his tractor around the hill following the old road. He moved out some of the rocks and fallen trees to make it easier to drive in. He even plowed through the big blackberry patches. When we got to the spring, Mod Snider, Hubert Grissom, Gilbert Hilton and Mr. Sam Smith were already there. As Elmer's obsession with the spring grew, so did the crowd.

After a few minutes, the backhoe has dug a hole all the way back into the mountain. Roots of the giant oak that stands a few yards from the spring are exposed. The backhoe operator gets off of the machine, and everyone looks deep into the mountain. Everyone, including me, looks for water. There ain't anything but a deep mud hole. The equipment operator says to the group, "There ain't no spring here anymore; there just ain't." He backed out of the hole and went home.

Elmer said, "I reckon it will take dynamite."

The group of men said, "Elmer, we are your friends; have been since we were children. But if-n you shoot that spring and our cisterns go to leaking, we will make you fix 'em."

Others said, "If you cause my well to go dry, I'll sue you to drill another well."

For a few weeks, Daddy still talked about dynamiting the spring. But, before too long, he just got the idea that the water was gone. Just like the old road was gone. People did not need the spring water any more. Times had changed, and that was all there was to it. The old spring was no more. That summer, the big oak tree died, too. I think it was because the backhoe dug up too many roots. Shorty said the old tree just thirsted to death. But the water did not come back to the spring.

That next spring, the holler and big ditch filled with dogwood and redbud flowers. The view of the New River was as pretty as ever. The cows and horses still went to the spring holler. Warm breezes still blew up the river, and the old spring was never mentioned again. Daddy never went back into the spring holler ever again. Me, I only went looking for the milk cow and the horse. All that digging and fuss changed things. If Elmer remembered the spring, he never let on.

"Things do change, and that is why you got your memories," my Grandmother explained.

Grandmother's Bowl

Go on and put this piece of wire in the smokehouse. It ain't no count, but it might be handy one day.

About the time Shorty and Grandmother gave me this bowl, it had been in her family for a long time. It all started on the day I set up housekeeping in the little cinderblock house down on New River. I did not have anything— not a bed, not a chair and not even a bowl.

This old bowl was not real important to Grandmother or anyone; it had a chip or two. (I do remember a time when it set on her dining room table.) But for some reason it seemed important to me. I have always kept it, because I think of her when I use it. Not more than a few years ago, one of my aunts asked me how I came to have this family antique. She is nearly 80 years old. "It is truly one of the old family heirlooms," she said. "When I was a child no more than eight or nine, we always served coleslaw and potato salad in this bowl or one just like it. I thought it had been lost or broken 50 years ago."

Now I keep this old yellow and green bowl in the cabinet and drag it out for family reunions.

I once thought that the past was dead and gone, never to be seen again. Well, the past is not dead at all. The past is resting comfortably in one of the back corners of our minds and comes up to the surface to be relived every once in a while. Like when an old lost potato-salad bowl is set on a table at the family reunion.

I now try to keep the old family relic in a safe place. One day I will pass it on to someone else. It will then vanish again from family recollection. Then, in 40 or 50 or 60 years, one of my cousins will say, "Where in the world did that old bowl come from? Is that Charles' old bowl that came from our great-grandmother's kitchen cabinet? I thought that it was lost 50 years ago. I just wonder where it came from, and how did he come by it?

"Well it ain't no count, but someday it might come in handy."

Dandelions

Aunt Virgie once told me, "A new broom will always sweep cleaner, but an old broom has experience and knows where the dirt is hiding."

Yes, I said dandelions. It is going to take a page or two to answer this question. For years, I have worked for the Virginia Extension Service. One of the fun things about my job was the people I met and the funny questions some of them once brought to my office. I do not care what the question was, they expected me to know the exact context, to understand their experience and to have an answer right now. One fine spring morning, a lady came to my office with bunch of dandelions in her hands. "How in the world does a person get rid of these things?" she queried.

Well, I talked with her about lawn-mowing practices and proper fertilization. I even suggested a herbicide that could be used on her lawn. She then asked me. "Well, how did older people control dandelions before lawn mowers and chemicals?"

To be honest, I do not know exactly how to answer this for sure; but for my grandmother and other older members of my family, dandelions were not a problem. On River Ridge, they were always a welcome sign of spring. Why? Because we ate and drank them. We ate the dandelion greens all spring and fried up the flowers and ate them too. Daddy and Shorty made lots of dandelion wine. Some of the old timers even pulled up the roots and made a coffee-like drink. Come to think of it, I liked all of this except the coffee-like concoction. That stuff is for only the toughest of men! You know, the World War II veterans and the like.

I went off to college one time, and here is one of the things I learned. We are talking about the regular old common dandelion or *Taraxacum officinale.* (I put that name in so you would not get them dandelions mixed up with other plants in your yard.) Dandelions were cultivated in Europe, and in America the Native Americans used them, too. Both cultures used dandelions for food and medicine. We surely ate a lot of them. But as for medicine, you are on your own to figure that out. About, the only thing that I think they cure is constipation. I can tell you for a fact that constipation ain't got a chance when fresh hot dandelion greens are eaten. No, not one chance in fifty, if you drink the bitter pot licker!!

In the spring on up into early summer, we all carried a folded up grocery bag about everywhere we went. When I stumbled across a patch of dandelions and other wild greens, I would stop and cut off the greens. Now Uncle Shorty and Elmer (Elmer was my father) did like the spring dandelion greens, and they ate a lot of them. But, they were always looking for the flowers they could use to make wine. If Mother or anyone else ran across a patch of flowers first, they brought them home to fry. Mamaw would make a thin pancake batter with no sugar and no vanilla. She would have a cast iron skillet of lard just steaming hot, then roll the dandelion flowers in the pancake batter and set them in the waiting lard. They fried up brown in just a few seconds. They were good. To me, they were a lot like a fried mushroom. Sometimes people still eat fried pumpkin flowers at high-dollar restaurants, but rarely do they try the dandelion flowers. The more flowers you ate, the fewer would go to seed.

We would pick two or three large buckets full of the green leaves. It took longer to wash them all than it did to pick them. In a very large stew pot, a large hunk of salt-cured fat meat was boiled. As soon as it was cooked, all of the dandelion greens were added to the boiling water and cooked until they were an unrecognizable pan of green stuff. The more you eat, the fewer can set flowers.

Oh yes, another thing one must do: clear the path to the outhouse of all obstacles. If you don't, somebody is going to get trampled, and you are going to make a big mess, because you are going to be running and I mean fast. Often people are going to be coming from different directions, too. So, I would always keep the toilet in sight.

I do remember my father, Uncle Shorty and Uncle Nelson all picking flowers, and my mother and all the wives on the hill being madder than hornets. I think they knew that in a month or so there was a time coming when the men on the hill were going to be hollering at the moon. Plus, the more flowers the men picked, the fewer greens they collected for eating. You do know that good wine does take precedence over eating. Well, that was my logic at the time.

When a very large pile of flowers had been heaped up under the big willow tree in Grandmother's backyard, men would set and pick all the yellow petals off the flowers. "If-n you put the whole dandelion plant in the wine, it will turn out to be sour," they'd all answer in unison, when I would ask why we were doing this.

One spring day, Daddy and Uncle Shorty and Nelson worked all day making homemade dandelion wine and home brew. Down in the barn loft, they had every crock covered with cheesecloth. I bet there was more than 20 gallons of stuff working. Every day they would meet at the barn to smell and taste their fermenting concoction and ever so slowly stir it. Every day the anticipation just grew. "This is going to be one of the best runs ever," they all would agree.

One morning my grandmother asked my mother if-n she was going off to town on the Old Cream Bus. "If-n you are," she insisted, "I have strong need for Ex-Lax and Black Drought."

Mother told Daddy that Grandmother was in a real bad way. "She must have been constipated for a month to need that much laxatives."

Well, Mother goes and buys out all the laxatives in the Mick or Mack Store and Piggly Wiggly. She comes home and gives the laxatives to Grandmother. In a day or two, Mother asked Mamaw how she was feeling. "Oh, just fine, never felt better," she replied. Mother now thinks, "Well, Mamaw has finally been able to go to the toilet."

The brothers started talking about bottling their brew on the coming Saturday. So, bright and early that day they set to washing out every old wine bottle, one-gallon vinegar jug, and anything else that would hold wine. They set everything out on the hog-scalding platform and started straining wine through a cheesecloth. Every once in a while, each would take a long big drink of their young new Dandelion Wine. After an hour or so of straining and sampling the new wine, it was put into the root cellar so it would stay cool and finish working off.

Mamaw always set on the front porch where she could watch what was going on. She knew more about the three houses (Elmer's, Nelson's and Shorty's) than the men did. Every day she just sat silently and watched. But today, there was something different. Every once in a while Daddy would break for the toilet like his hat was on fire. Then Uncle Nelson would start out over the bank to his toilet just like he was on roller skates. You could hear Uncle Shorty running through the house and knocking the screen door open. All were screaming for the right of way. They had to shit, and I mean right now. My mother, Ruth, came around the corner of the house and caught Mamaw just laughing! Mother said, "Her belly fat was just a-jumping up and down. She had laughed until her nose was running like a sugar tree in the spring, and she was coughing a lot. too."

"What in the world is so funny?" Momma asked.

Without talking, Mamaw pointed at the next man running for the toilet almost tearing off his bibbed overhauls as he screamed for a clear path. Now, she had awful bad arthritis. So bad in fact that she had a lot of trouble making it to the toilet on her own. She walked slowly and kind of rocked back and forth on the sore legs. She told Mother, "Well, I heard them talk about their home brew so much, that I thought that I would just have the last laugh out of this. Ruth, do you remember all those laxatives? Well, when everyone was at work, I worked my way down over the hill to the barn and dumped laxatives in each of their crocks. I stirred it around real careful so as not to mix up the drags in the bottom. I gave them all the Running Trots."

Daddy was so sick that he just lay in the yard with an ice bag on his head. Mother made a picture of his sickness. When it dawned on her what had happened, she told each man that their wine had been spiked with Ex-Lax and to stop drinking it. You see, they would crap and then go drink up more of the wine. Daddy said it was so bad that, "Hell I thought I was going to fill up the toilet, if-n I lived long enough that is." Mother went and told Mamaw to never draw her into another one of her son-killing schemes.

Well, after the story was out, no one took care of the leftover gallons of home brew and wine. In a few days, it exploded all over the cellar floor. That place stunk like fresh wine, then rotten wine and finally like something I do not want to smell again. Everyone worked on cleaning up the mess. Poor Old Elmer would just retch and cough and spit a lot, but he got through it.

You may be thinking that would stop the home-brew making? The answer is NO. They just went back to looking for new bottles. They had to hurry, too. Mulberries would be coming in just a few days. Raspberries and blackberries would be ripe soon, and wine-making would start up again.

My suggested treatment for your dandelions is, a soil sample, proper lawn fertility, mow your grass at least three inches high. Use a chemical control if you need to or just eat them dandelions. Another way is just to admire the yellow flowers, because they are here to stay.

Momma and Her Bologna Bowls

A common expression on River Ridge was, "Sometimes it is better to have dumb luck on your side than to be right."

Not long before Mother died, she asked me to fix her a plate of bologna bowls. It is funny what we remember when it comes to food! Most people have never heard of such a thing as a bologna bowl. But I have, and I do remember them from my childhood. Also, there is no truer statement than what goes around comes around.

When I was a little kid, we ate a lot of bologna. Daddy and Momma would purchase a ten-pound roll, we often called a "hank of bologna." We ate bologna biscuits, fried bologna, and sandwiches. Often, Momma would fry bologna for breakfast and make a real thick brown gravy. Bologna, eggs and gravy were a River Ridge favorite. Just hearing those words makes me want to head for the refrigerator. Bologna sandwiches with red tomatoes and mayonnaise were a favorite summertime meal, too.

But one of my mother's all-time favorite bologna meals was what she called "bologna bowls." Please let me explain how you make this Lytton favorite, and I can just bet that you will run to the refrigerator. First, you fry up your bologna so that it curls up in the pan, forming a bowl. When the fat starts to accumulate in the pan, you set the curled up bologna out on a dish. Into the bologna drippings you add flour and slowly stir it until it is cooked brown, then add enough milk. Stir and simmer until it is real thick gravy. Make a large pan of mashed potatoes. Once the gravy is hot, and the bologna curled up, add a large spoon of mashed potatoes to each piece of curled bologna. Then place three or four bologna bowls on your plate. Pour the gravy around the bologna-filled slices until the gravy is just about to the top of the curled bologna, and eat away.

Recently, I stopped at a local fast-food restaurant for my morning sausage biscuit. The lady at the counter said, "Can I interest you in a fresh, homemade bologna biscuit?" I answered, "Only if you can put eggs on it, and can give me two." I ate them every day for at least a week. Everything that goes around comes around. As for the bologna gravy, once or twice in 50 years is enough. But, I still think about fried bologna. A country music singer once wrote a song about being in jail in Roanoke, Virginia, and being fed fried bologna, eggs and gravy.

Sadly, I did not make Mother the bologna bowls. Why, I cannot answer. But I did take her a few of the hot, fresh, homemade Bologna biscuits from the fast-food restaurant. "They are good," Mother said.

Where Did Them Lyttons Come from Anyway

When looking for a job, what you know don't mean nothing! If you get the job, it is who you know. So always shake everybody's hand.

First, to understand where I came from you must understand where the Lyttons started. To be honest here, I don't have a lot of details. Grandmother was a Dehart from River Ridge and Granddad Ervin Oakley Lytton was from near Radford or Walton or somewhere over in those parts. One story said that his family lived near the community of Vickers Switch not too far from the Virginian Railroad Water Tank. He was born September 21, 1882, in Montgomery County, Virginia, and he died March 3, 1929, still in Montgomery County (at the age of 47). His world was really small. Much like a wild deer, he never went more than 25 or 30 miles in any direction from his birthplace.

Irene May Dehart was born February 10, 1889, in Franklin County, Virginia. She died in Montgomery County October 17, 1983, (at 94). Mamaw's world was much larger.

She started life in a time when it required a five-day horse-drawn wagon's trip to Christiansburg to pay taxes and lived to watch men take a five-day space ride to the moon. She rode trains and buses, too. She never rode in an airplane and never said much about it, either. Maybe she didn't want to, I am thinking.

Her parents were my Great Grandmother Adelaide Bowles Dehart and Great Granddaddy Rufus Dehart, who lived in Franklin County, Virginia, until somewhere around 1900 when they moved to the holler just below my homeplace.

Somewhere along the way I need to sit down and tell you all about Rufus Dehart and the two secret lives he lived. Hollywood could make Old Rufus' life into a bestselling movie. Well heck, I will give you a sentence or two on him right now. I think that this was very hard real-life training for my grandmother. I do want to reserve the right be wrong a little bit here, because all of this took place 50 or 60 years before I was born, and I did not see any of it. I only heard stories about these people. All of my information is secondhand; some is even thirdhand. If you have more information, now would be a good time to tell it.

Great Grandmother Adelaide for the most part raised her family by herself. You see, Old Rufus was given to being a rambler. He would leave River Ridge and be gone for three and four months at a time. One of my aunts said that he only lived on River Ridge for six months at a time at most, and then the rambling urge would hit him. Much later on, we learned that he had a second family in West Virginia. He would visit them for a few months and then come back to River Ridge. Another one of my aunts said he stayed at home, on River Ridge, just long enough to get Adelaide pregnant before he left again.

Now, here is just a part that Grandmother Irene May — "Mamaw" — told me many years ago. I do not have any data to back this up. Adelaide and Rufus moved after a moonshine dispute erupted in Franklin County. This must have been in the very late 1890s. Grandmother said they ran a distillery and were on the losing side of the dispute and had to move. One of my aunts insisted that they were just common old moonshiners and bootleggers. Others aunts and uncles said their grandparents had worked in a legal and bonded bourbon distillery in Franklin County. Now, you can believe what you want here. As for me, I have only heard of the moonshine side of Franklin County, and I question the idea there was a legal still anywhere in those parts. Grandmother told me, though, that as a child she carried buckets of hot mash away from the large stills to the hogs. "The hogs were big, fat and drunk from eating the hot mash, but the animals just loved the cooked grain," she said.

After her family moved to River Ridge and bought the homeplace, Grandmother, then a young lady, worked across the river in the Flannigans' house. To get to work, she either paddled a boat across the river each day or walked the river road to Whitethorn and rode the ferry. Granddad Ervin already worked on the same farm. (The Flannigan Farm is currently the Radford Arsenal property.) When they met and married, Irene May was 16 and Ervin was a little older.

They started married life down in the holler below the barn at Adelaide and Rufus' house, and eventually had 10 children of their own, five boys and five girls. Later, after the new road was built, Irene and Ervin moved out of May's Holler up onto the ridge and built a new home for themselves. This house still stands.

I never saw the old place down in the hollow with my own eyes, but I did get a glimpse of it from Mamaw's stories. I only saw small pieces of the burnt remains, the small stack of old foundation rocks and an old bed frame placed over a crumbling cistern. The house backed up to the hillside near the big Stayman apple tree in the holler. There was a very large catalpa tree in the corner of the front yard and a large apple tree in the back.

I can remember Daddy and Uncle Shorty picking up rocks from the potato patch and pitching them down the old cistern so livestock would not fall in and break a leg. The main thing I can remember is the giant catalpa tree and big apple in the backyard that once shaded the house. Even those childhood memories are failing me now. Uncle Shorty had a large hog lot that came up to the edge of the old cistern. He would pull buckets of water out for the hogs.

After Great Grandmother Adelaide died of cancer in the old house, about all of my aunts and uncles said the place just smelled sick. No one liked going into the sick house. One late evening in the fall it just caught on fire. No one could tell me much about how. One aunt said, "The old house was a sick place, and it had to be burnt to the ground to clean up the smell and mess." I reckon the old house was full of old ghosts and bad memories. I find it funny as I set here this evening; neither Daddy, Shorty nor Nelson ever had much to say about the old homeplace. In a way it was just gone; even the old ghost, too. The old apple tree was cut up for firewood more than 30 years ago.

The Old Road

The old road came down from Prices Fork, dodging the sinkholes, staying in the woods over close to the cliff. If you use your imagination a little as you drive up the McCoy Road, you can make out sections of the older McCoy Road as it meanders through the fields and woods. It was built before the 30s. But there was a road built even before that one. The section right behind Mamaw's house was referred to as "The road down by the old junk car" or "The road to the trash pile."

This ancient road was partway made some time back in the 1800s. I guess it started out as a footpath. Later people with horses walked the path. Uncle Lake told me that "cowboys" lived on River Ridge, too. But, they were not the kind that was in the TV shows. Every fall farmers got together and started walking their calves to market. Some were walked toward Prices Fork and others to the train station in Whitethorne. So I guess livestock also pounded out the Old Road. I have been told the Union troops also walked down this old ancient road on their way to Whitethorne Farm during the American Civil War. I find it most curious that today older people ask me where the old road was.

There was an old Dodge car that Mamaw's youngest brother, Delmar, had wrecked and horses had dragged in and just left sitting there in the steep curve to rust away. While it was rusting, we dumped trash beside it. For many hours, I practiced my driving sitting behind the steering wheel with rusty seat springs poking me in the butt. The broken windshield folded down on the hood. I had a clear view of my future as a car driver, and I was fast, real fast in that old wrecked car.

I asked Mamaw why in the world the road builders took such a meandering way when a straight line would have been much easier. "Pasture grass and open ground that a farmer could work was at a premium. Country people don't have anywhere to go anyway, so why build much of road," she answered. "Plus, there was very few big trees back then, and the road was setting over at the edge of woods."

From the old junk car, the road curved up the hill near where the barn once stood. Then the road went out around the hill and turned down into the holler above where the pond is, but just at the lower edge of Uncle Nelson's hog lot. Then it made a sharp turn toward the New River. Just before the railroad gate it turned right up over the hill, then followed the railroad to where the railroad crossing is today, and just followed the river on to Whitethorne. Daddy and my uncles said the river section of road was open long after the railroad was built. But blasting through the "Yellow Rock Cut" pitched large rocks over the bank and partially blocked the river road to wagons and cars. Still, people walked up the Snider bottom to fish and visit. Another thing, the new road to Whitethorne was almost finished, and the river road wasn't needed anymore.

Once upon a time, I loved to harness our horse and hook him to the wooden sled. I always used the small sled with the wooden runners. "That sled will do all you are going to do," Uncle Shorty would tell me. I went from our house to Uncle Nelson's and Grandmother's picking up all the household trash to take to the old car. Grandmother said that when I came down the path with the horse it made her think back to when she was a young girl and almost all the traffic on the old road was horses and wagons and people walking. Then one day there were no wagons, just slow cars. Soon the gates dividing people's fields and properties were replaced with wire fences, and the road was gone.

What I remember best about the old homeplace in the holler is the orchard. There were three pear trees and more than five kinds of apple trees. I like the two early harvest apple trees, one kind of red and the other yellow, just like the one next to the old store in Price's Fork. Each summer when apples are ripe and falling, I stop and pick up one or two just to remember my youth. Down in the holler, I would eat them until my stomach hurt. Man they were sweet! About 15 or 20 years ago I found an apple seedling in the hollow. I pulled it up and planted it at the family cemetery. It turned out to be the last of the early harvest red apples. Now I fight with worms, rabbits and deer to eat a few bites each year. They are still good and packed full of Grandmother's stories!!

As a child I climbed the trees over by the cliff near the railroad in search of the best of the best apples. I learned early that the best ones are right in the top where the sun and wind have had their way with them. I think my favorite apple was from a tree that Uncle Delmar was said to have planted. Mamaw said her brother had eaten this apple somewhere on one of his many short travels and brought home the seeds in his pocket. He planted some seeds on the cliff down below the barn and some on the path from Mamaw's house to Uncle Nelson's. Everyone called it a "Smokehouse" apple. Most likely these were either York or Stayman apples. In the fall they were as hard as a rock, but by New Year's they'd be soft and mellow. They were known all over the world and River Ridge as "Fried Pie Apples." From a seed to apple-bearing may take 15 to 20 years. By my time, in the 1950s and 1960s, they were giant apple trees. Today even their stumps have long since rotted away. But I still know where they were and how they tasted.

When I was eight or nine, Grandmother would ask me to harness the horse, Fanny, hook her to the small wooden sled and go to the holler to sled back apples. I never got to drive the four-wheel, horse-drawn wagon. "Hell, boy, that thing will get away from you and kill you and scratch up them horses," Daddy, Uncle Shorty and Uncle Nelson would tell me. Somehow I did not think they were worried about me that much.

Well, anyway, when I got back with a sled of apples,

33

we made them into fried pies, applesauce and apple butter. The real hard ones we put in the cellar for eating around Christmastime. We also ate thousands of them cut into pieces and covered with salt. Grandmother always seemed to know when I was coming, because she would fry up hard apples and canned sausage just for me to eat. I always ate my fill, too. The more I ate, the more she and Uncle Shorty laughed and the more they shoved a plate toward me.

There on River Ridge, Grandmother had a little farm of about 25 total acres. The McCoy Road passed in the front, and the Virginian Railroad and New River in the back. Granddaddy Ervin had died when their youngest child was six months old.

According to the story, one day he got his new denim jacket hung in the ladder going into the caboose as the train headed up the mountain toward Pepper. He was dragged part of the way before he got himself loose, and he was never very healthy after that. In 1929, when he died, he left my grandmother the job of raising the 10 kids. A sad truth is she knew what to do, since she had seen her mother take on the same job.

Mamaw just had the Great Depression to deal with. When she would tell stories she would say to me, "Thank the Good Lord for these 25 acres." On the little farm, we grew hogs, a few milk cows and horses. Grandmother once said, "The cows were for milk and butter and beef for selling. Mountain people eat pork; only town people can afford to eat much beef. That is one of the ways you can tell us apart." I reckon even in her day there were townies and country boys.

As I have listened to these stories through the years, the toughness of this bunch rings throughout. I sometimes wonder what it must have been like in that house. There must have been something going on all of the time. I do think that each and every one of them came from very strong stock. I think the Dehart-Lytton cross yielded some very remarkable people.

Mr. Mod Snider told me once that Uncle Nelson looked the most like Grandmother's brother, Bayard, who worked the Big Vein Coal Mine in McCoy. Mod said Great Uncle Bayard was one of the most powerfully strong men he had ever seen, and he had several stories to prove the point. One time when the mules balked with a load of coal, Bayard put his full weight behind it, and the coal car started to move again. Another time one of the little coal cars ran off the track, and five or six men gathered along the side to "give a lift." They were not able to put the car back on the track. Bayard yelled, "Someone here ain't giving all they got." No one answered. Bayard said, "Well, by jingos, it must be me then." The next lift the coal car was set back on the track. Mr. Mod Snider told me that I had a lot of Dehart in me. Others would tell me this, too. As I look in the mirror, I guess they were talking about my great gift of good looks; I do seem to be right pretty.

Anyway, I think that all of the Lyttons, both aunts and uncles, had one thing in common. Living on River Ridge they had a right hard life that required them to earn a living each and every day. If they did not work, they did not eat; it was as simple as that. I also think that they kind of grew up as best they could by making up their own rules for life as they went along. Godfrey Hill told me this more than once. To hear others tell it, the Lyttons weren't given to fighting and arguing much, but they did not take much guff either. They just stayed to themselves and worked because they had to.

Even today, I still wander along the old roadbed just to think back to those that walked it long before me. I think back on those aunts and uncles that I never met. I wonder how I would shape up among them?

The Sacred Order
of the Golden Dragon

If you want to get ahead in this life you need to be the one looking for the path.

Harman Elmer Lytton, my father, went by many names. Some called him "Pickle." I asked, but no one could tell me where "Pickle" came from. Others called him "Mole." Uncle Fred once said that Daddy would sit outside in the yard, in the spring sun, for hours watching for moles to run through their dens. Once he saw the ground move, he'd pounce so quickly that it would make your head swim. I cannot see Pappy jumping up that fast for anything except a good glass of cold buttermilk and some cornbread or a long, slow drink of sour-mash whiskey. Now, he liked that. Truth is, so do I, especially if it is homemade sour mash.

I think that my father knew that he was about to die. A week or so before his death, we were setting in the back room of the house talking, when all of a sudden he got real quiet. When he finally spoke again, he asked me to take his Sacred Order of the Golden Dragon certificate from the wall. He dusted it with his arm and handed it to me. "Here, I want you to take this. This proves that I was in World War II. Please take it and keep it. That war was hard on me and on everyone else, too. But, somehow I did it and somehow I made it."

I'm pretty sure that Daddy saw this as his most prized accomplishment in life. The certificate indicates the time and date his ship crossed the International Dateline. Again, proof that he had truly seen the world, or, as he frequently said, "I have sailed all over the seven seas and every ocean and gone for days and weeks without seeing any land." He was always proud of that.

Just a few weeks ago, I received an envelope from the family lockbox down at the bank. Among the letters were a few medical statements from the military. Once I looked at them, I learned that my father had a very hard time dealing with World War II. It is amazing what he kept locked in his heart and mind away from the world and us kids.

Today, I keep his Sacred Order of the Golden Dragon certificate over my dresser. Every morning, when I look at it, I just wonder what I will have accomplished in my time on this earth. . .and what I'll leave behind as my placeholder. . .and if someone will remember my ever being here. I think that someday, you just never know, I might write a book! That might be my placeholder.

Mom and Dad

A chicken don't brag any when he is in the soup.

Harmon Elmer Lytton, my dad, was a local boy through and through. He was born on River Ridge and raised there and died there. As I wrote before, he went by many names. Ruth Alma Millington was a different story. Mom was a Richmond native, and she had only one name—Ruth. Daddy was a lifelong Democrat, and Franklin Roosevelt could not do anything wrong. Mom was a tried and true follower of the Republican Party. Long live Herbert Hoover. I asked Mom once about this political family situation, and she had a quick answer: "You can listen all you want to people, but when the curtain is drawn on the voting booth you are free to do what is good and right and proper." I guess she voted how she wanted!

How the two ever got together and stayed together is a mystery to me. As the story was told to me, after World War II both Uncle Fred and Daddy were working on construction in Richmond. Believe it or not, Daddy was a steelworker and enjoyed working high off the ground. "The higher you went the better the pay," he claimed. Fred had a girlfriend named Betty who worked with Ruth at the DuPont Plant in Richmond. Fred and Betty fixed Elmer and Ruth up on a blind date. When the four of them went on a picnic, Daddy ate some potato salad, and remarked, "I just might marry the lady that made this potato salad." The rest is just part of family history.

After Mom and Daddy married, they lived and worked in Charlottesville, Virginia, moving around the area from one construction site to another. They did not move back to River Ridge until Mom was pregnant with my sister. As Mom remembered it, Grandmother told Daddy to come home so the baby could be born with her family. There are differing stories about his move. You see, like many youngest sons, Daddy was a whole lot spoiled by Grandmother. For the remainder of her life she still told him what to do. For many years, this was a major bone of contention between Ruth and Elmer.

As for Mother's family, I only met my Grandfather and Grandmother Millington a few times, and it was when I was very young. They seemed to be real nice people. But Uncle Tony was about the only member of Mother's family I truly ever knew, and I did not know too much about him. I do remember a Christmas present he once gave me, when I was about four or five years old. It was a seven-piece model of a human skull and brain. If you got all of the pieces put together just right, it would slip down into a life-size plastic skull and you could put the scalp on it. Now, I just think or thought that it was plastic; it might have been real, for all I know. In any case, I was not looking at that thing any more than I had too. Once I saw the thing, I could not sleep for a week. I would hide this head of a thing every once in a while, and my life got a little easier. "Where did it go?" Mom would ask. I never told anyone, but I put it in the bottom of the chiffarobe, or I hid it under the back of the steps heading to down into the basement. Then out of nowhere, someone would find it again. The skull and brain would just sit on the shelf and look right at you with those empty eye sockets.

I guess I was basically raised by Daddy's family right there on River Ridge. Everyone had a given name and a given nickname. Everyone in the whole community would use your nickname as often as your real name. About 15 years ago, I stopped in at Long Shop Service Center and Miss Nancy Albert was there. She said that sometime back she had seen one of my brothers or sisters and had been trying to remember all of the bear names. Now I think that is funny. We were all named after bears; my bear name was "Car-Starting Bear."

Mother, She Is a Real Jewel

Once in a while Mom would say to me, "Be careful where you walk. There are things worse than holes to step in."

In our family, Mom was the strong one. For the most part, she was a stay-at-home mom, and she kept everything moving. To my knowledge she did go to public work two times. The first was when the house was being built. I was about three or four and don't recall too much of that time. This was because Daddy fell into the cistern and broke his neck for the second time. While he was recuperating, the bills took to piling up, so she went to work at the sewing factory in Christiansburg.

She worked on piecework and made little money, but worked very hard. On River Ridge, work on the house just stopped and never got started again. Through the years, I would see Mom unroll the original drawings for the house she so badly wanted and had dreamed of. She complained very softly, and her tears were small ones. "You children are what is important to me now," softly she would say to me. Later on, she would tell me that your life and dreams can change in one second. So be careful where you walk!

The second time Mama went to work, the family was getting behind on bills. She took a job as a cook in the school cafeteria. She was a good cook! I did not like this job too much, because she always rode my school bus home. This cut down on my loud socializing and picking at others. Mamma tried real hard to pay no attention to me, but sometimes she just could not help it.

If it was time to kill hogs, she was ready. When we were plowing the garden, she had the seed packs and a hoe. She made a lot of our clothes and could turn a printed feed sack into a great shirt. I can remember her and Grandmother going with us to the feed store. She picked out hog feed by the design on the sacks. Once in a while I would be embarrassed to wear a feed-sack shirt to school. Even back in my youth, most people wore store-bought clothes out in public. I soon learned that with seven mouths to feed, you made every feed sack count. Today, I think a cotton feed-sack shirt would be great. After reading this section, one of my cousins told me that his mother told him that her underwear was even made by our grandmother.

Mom was a character, too. I can remember one time when one of my cousins had gotten a small mini-bike. A whole group of us were sitting on the front porch of the house when he made a trip around the yard and then another macho family boy took a turn. Mom was not to be outdone, so she jumped on and away she went. I guess I should have told you that Mom had a hairbraid on her head that was more than four feet long and as big around as a ball bat. Another important part in this story is that she had not ridden a bicycle in 40 years. Since she had never been on a mini-bike ever, she had not one clue how to stop it or make it go and knew little about how to steer the machine.

Mom took off through the front yard as fast as the bike would go, heading straight for the hardtop. Just before the hardtop there was a row of very large flowering quince bushes complete with lots of limbs and lots of thorns. With that big, long braid loose and just a-flopping behind her, she never tried to stop or even slow down. She went straight into the hedgerow. The flowering quince scratched her unmercifully and held onto her—by the hair. She was going just like Casey Jones; both of them kept their hand on the throttle. The little machine was running wide open and just a-digging. Mom was hollering, "How do you cut the damn thing off?" We all ran after her, and we had to use hedge clippers cut her out.

Another time, Mom went down to feed the hog and fell headfirst into the hog chop barrel. When she fell, the barrel was all but empty, and she was reaching almost to the bottom to get to the hog feed. I would have loved to have seen that or her getting out, but I did not. Mom said that she was standing on her head in the barrel and had to rock the barrel back and forth to get it to tip over. "It hurt like hell, too, and that damn chop is dry and tastes awful. The more I would rock, the deeper my head sunk in the chop. I thought that I was going to be drowned in hog feed." She broke a few ribs, but she did not tell anyone for a long time. The next day, she drove to Richmond and back with the broken ribs.

One of the funniest things I ever saw in my whole life was Mom drunk. She never drank beer, wine, or whiskey. She did not like it, though she did like to pick the grapes from the vine in the backyard to make grape wine. Daddy was different. He would drink about anything from home brew to hen peck to moonshine. His only criterion was there had to be a lot of it. Well, one weekend Dad had drunk up a lot of booze and stayed drunk all weekend. Mom had had about all she could put up with. Her solution was to show him just how bad he looked when he was drunk.

When she drank half a gallon or more of her homemade wine, everything went well for about the first 10 or 15 minutes. Then the world started to turn, and she took to her bed. Her plan was quickly falling to pieces. She got really sick. To say the least, she ditched her cookies or grape juice all over the house. Maybe as much as two or three gallons came out of her; there could have been four gallons, I am not sure. She did this in a most unladylike fashion. She held onto the wall and started upchucking. It made me sick to watch. I washed her face and got her back on the bed. I cleaned up her mess. I ditched my cookies outside once or twice. Mom thought that she was going to pass over the great river, and I do not mean the Potomac.

When Elmer learned of Mother's wine-drinking, he got

mad at her. "The very idea of you, their mother, getting drunk in front of my children," he said. It was okay for him to get drunk and stagger around like a circus clown, but not her. He could be a sexist ass, I reckon.

Mom and Dad had grown accustomed to keeping the kids close to home. At the time a lot of people did this. We often heard about polio. Two young people on our road had polio, and our parents did everything they could to keep us away from large groups of people. We did lots of stuff as a family. We went swimming in the creek. We made picnics on the riverbank. Sometimes we took drives around the New River Valley. Elmer was famous for stopping at the store and getting each family member a moon pie, a hunk of cheese and a Royal Crown Cola (an RC). Now, for us, these drives were just great. Mom was always trying to look out for us the best way she could. Mothers are like that, I guess.

About the meanest thing I ever did was "skeer" my mother. One bright day, a big Black Racer went through the backyard. He was so black the sun made his scales shine almost blue. The snake must have been every bit of six feet long and as big around as a hoe handle. Yes sir, he was fine, a handsome snake. Where he came from is still up for debate; where he was going I have no clue. But Ruth thought that he was just so ugly and something to be so afraid of that she took off running for the house and left me looking at where the snake went. Truth is, she forgot me and left me standing like a lost ball in the high weeds. Only after she was in the house did she look out the window and holler for me to come on.

Well, a few days later Mom was washing clothes and had the basement window open. As I walked past the window, I got the bright idea of testing just how skeered of snakes she really was. So, I decided to just sneak up beside the house, take off my belt and pitch it through the open window. The belt hit Mom, and she took to screaming and trembling. She tried to run, but her feet just didn't answer, so she just kind of hopped real fast-like, in one place. Then she started to let out a real pitiful moan. You know, kind of like the sound you make when the milk cow is standing on your foot and will not move over. Then, she just started to cry with more long pitiful moans.

I went running into the basement and found her with her head leaning up on the wall still just crying real loud. She was also standing in a puddle of pee. She was not happy, either. Once she got through peeing her britches and crying, she took out after me, and when she caught up to me she lit into me with the first stick she could find. She was hopping mad, I am telling you. "You little shit ass! Don't you ever do that to me again. Why, you made me pee my britches." Yes, that is what she called me. The cussing was real, and switching was real too, as was the pee.

Mom was a great cook, too! The best thing she cooked was homemade biscuits. She said that when she moved to the mountains she could not make a biscuit worth a damn. They always looked like a thick, real hard cracker. They would not or could not soak up any butter or gravy. Apple butter just set up

47

on top and looked back at you. They were so bad that she just wanted to cry. Grandmother told her, "Just don't fret none, little girl. You just come back after you have made two regular-size railroad cars full. I can just bet you will be better."

As we got older, Mom started up a little gambling ring. We played penny-ante poker for hours on end, keeping everyone's winnings in different jars. She always kept new cards for us. We must have played a million games of Rook, as well. Again, she always kept the cards and didn't let us get too rowdy. She did not think much of us going off to other people's houses, but she always welcomed our friends. Some of these people came and grew to be as close as brothers and sisters. They still are, too!

Also, when we got to be older still, she bought a new ice crusher each week. In the summer, we got to playing croquet in the front yard. We would drink daiquiris and play croquet from daylight to dark. We honestly wore out an ice crusher every Saturday and Sunday. We would pitch it over the hill, and Mom would go get another one.

Mr. Mod Snider would be there as soon as the dew lifted off the grass and not leave until the dew fell again. Sometimes we even played by car lights. Mod was one of the best. He played great croquet and smoked little cherry-smelling cigars. "Cawliga, you old wooden head, just watch this," he would say, meaning it for all of us. We would cheat like dogs and laugh at how badly we played the game. But, people came from everywhere to play. Mod loved to tell me about how they played croquet when he was a boy. He also regularly insisted: "This is just a game and games ain't ever worth getting mad over." I tell people the same thing to this day!

One of the best ones on my mother came a year or two before her death. She was living in a local nursing home. One of the upcoming activities was a display of the "lives of the residents." Mom asked me to help her put together a picture display of her life. Well, I show up with box of old black and white pictures that I have collected from homes all over River Ridge. I have a large cardboard display piece, too. Almost all the pictures were taken long before I was born. I know no one. So she slowly starts to sort them out and name the people in each picture. She puts them on the display board in the order and location she wants.

Well, there was this one picture Mother explained as "two handsome men." When we glued the picture to the display I asked, "Mom, who are the men in the picture?"

My 91-year-old mother just started to laugh, "The one on the left is Bill, and the one on the right is Johnny. Back in 1946, I was courting both of them right heavy." She broke into tears laughing and shaking. "Your old mother wasn't always this old, and both men were as sharp as a blade." The only other "blade" she spoke of was Paul Harris. A blade was a handsome man.

Mother and the Judge

When Mom was, I am guessing, near 80 years old, I get a call that she has been involved in a car accident. "She's just fine, a little bruised, but the car is a total loss," the caller stated. Well, I drive down to the house, and there she sets. She is in one bad mood. "I did it and it is all my fault. I pulled out right in front of that little girl," Mom informed me. "I have this ticket, too. I can just bet that the judge will never let me drive again! Is that what he is going to do?"

"I do not know," I answer. In the back of my mind I am thinking, "At your age you need to stop driving anyway." But I am not going to say anything like this. More than once, over the course of my life, I have seen Ruth Lytton get mad. I am too weak to see her get loud again. "Mom, I have no clue what the judge is going to say or do. Heck, he not might even do a thing," I answer.

Mama answered back, "Like hell. . .expletive, expletive,

expletive." Well obviously, that was the wrong answer.

Over the next few weeks Mom falls deeper into quiet. Her face is drawn with depression or something. She is very upset with herself for the wreck. She is very scared that the judge is going to tell her that she cannot drive anymore. She is also scared that this wreck is going to cost her a lot of money. She even gets to where she sets in the house with the lights off. Then, as the day for court draws closer, she cuts the light back on and perks up. She has made her mind up that she is just going to live with the judge's decision, and that is that.

We go to court. The judge is sitting behind a bench that is about my chest height. Someone calls Mother's name, and we stand up and walk to the front of the court. The judge looks at us and asks, "Who are you?"

I say, "This is my mother, and I came with her for her day in court." I take a few steps to her side. I want her to know that I am still with her.

Both the officer and the girl whose car was hit in the wreck explain what happened. While they are talking, Mom moves slowly, almost as if it's without motion, right to the edge of the judge's bench. Without a word, she raises up to full height and sets her chin right on the bench. Both the officer and victim pause and kind of start talking on Mom's behalf. When they stop talking, with no request from the judge, Mom says, "Your Honor, I am guilty as charged." She just loved to speak in complete sentences, and I just know that she has practiced this statement in her mind all morning.

The judge does not say a word for a few seconds, then raises up on his feet and bends over his bench. The judge's nose and Mother's nose are no more than one foot apart. "Mrs. Lytton, I think that you have already been punished enough. Mr. Lytton (that is me), please drive your mother home."

Well, we do not go home. We go looking for a new car! Mom and I visited two or three car lots and looked at and set in a number of cars. Salesmen would ask, "You all want to take this one for a drive?"

"No, I am just looking today." Then she would tell her story.

I think that Mom truly wanted a car and wanted to drive again. She was just letting her nerves settle down some and wanting her family to give some kind of approval.

After a week or so Mom finally settled on a new car. "This one, I like a lot. It is small, and I can see over the hood," she told the salesman. "I will take this one."

She was happier than I had seen her since the wreck. "I never ever even got say one word on purchasing a car before. Elmer always said it was a man's thing, and men make much better decisions on cars."

"Well, Mom, I kind of like this one too." In the back of my mind I was hoping that this deal would fall through!

The salesman came out of the dealership with magnetic license tags and a set of keys. He handed me the keys. I handed them to Mom. She got behind the wheel, and the salesman told me, "Take the car for a ride and see what you think."

"No sir, this is between you and Mother. She is the one purchasing the car, not me."

Mother had not driven in more than a month. In my opinion, and mine alone, she was kind of a sketchy driver before the wreck, and without much practice and in an unfamiliar car she just might be rusty.

Truly, she finally got the car started, and the salesman looked in the window at me with a real long look on his face, and then climbed in the back seat. On the road we went, and in a few minutes Mom pulled back into the car lot and parked the car in the same spot she left from.

She looked like a pro. The salesman got out of the car and went straight to his desk and sat down hard. He looked a little queasy and kind of peaked. Mother followed right along behind him. Once the paper work was completed, he handed Mom the keys, and she took out of the parking lot like she was going to a house fire.

The salesman looked at me and said, "What have we done?" Then, with a strange look on his face,, "Have you ever ridden with her?"

"Why, yes, I have; she'll be ok."

Within a short amount of time, Mom gave the car to her granddaughter. I honestly think she knew it was her time to stop driving. She just wanted to make up her own mind as to when she was going to stop.

When she handed over the keys, there was a collective slight sigh of relief up and down the Long Shop Road. Everybody was always looking out for Mom. That is just the way people are on River Ridge.

I just wonder if I'll know when to give someone else the keys?

Your Daddy Was a Good Eater

Everything looks nice and green when the goose is looking down. But up close, it ain't always so pretty and green.

Someone not long ago asked me why I am so big and right manly developed? My best start on this answer is locked up in this story. Mr. Buckshot ran a small Grade "C" dairy not too far from my home on River Ridge. He made his living milking about 20 to 25 cows by hand. He milked two times each and every day, seven days a week, almost all of his life. Yes, his hands were so tough that his fingers would not straighten out all the way, but he could crack your hand each time he shook it.

Because he ran a Grade "C" Dairy, he had to have a good springhouse, and it stayed very cool in there, around about 50 degrees or so, the temperature of the cool spring water coming straight out of the earth. He had no refrigeration like big modern dairies do. The inside of the springhouse was no more than 15 feet by 15 feet. The water was kept at a depth of about 12 to 14 inches. All of his milk was poured into metal milk cans that sat on the gravel floor surrounded by water for cool storage. In a day or two, the milk cans would be carried out and set on the side of the road for shipment. Another thing, some milk was stored in small earthen crocks, which often were full of cream set aside for home use.

More than once, on hot summer days, Mr. Buckshot said that they caught Daddy lying down in the cold water in the milk house with only his chest above the water line. He would have a milk crock turned up drinking the cream off the top. Fannie Lynn said "You could not set a pie out there to cool either; he would eat that, too."

Now, a lesser of a man just not could do this. A real man has got to eat and drink, doesn't he, if he is to grow properly with good teeth and a sound body foundation? Well, it is starting to look like Elmer is truly my father after all. We sure do favor a lot both in shape and eating habits. As for me, I can just see Elmer lying down in the cold water sipping the cream off of a crock and eating half of a pie. He must have been really hot and thirsty. I heard Mr. Buckshot picking at Daddy one day about his cabbaging off cold cream, and Daddy just kind of chuckled.

Shorty and Old Jim

Now, when Old Jim was not sleeping in the cabin, in Mom's house, Mr. Luther's barn or somebody's car, he slept in Shorty's barn. He would burrow deep up in the hay and wallow out a nice nest. If Uncle Shorty found him, he ran him out and nailed boards up over the door. He said, "That worthless damn hound is sapping all of the strength out of the hay. The more I feed the cow, the less milk she is giving."

I think the reason the horse or cows did poorly with the hay was because the hay was all real rough and about half weeds and blackberry briars and maybe more than half fescue hay. But poor Old Jim had to take the blame for it. I think it hurt the dog's feelings, too. I have to confess, though, I did like to see and hear about the ongoing battle between Old Jim and Shorty.

About once a week in the winter, up over the hill would come Uncle Shorty with poor Old Jim tied on a hay string. "You got to do something about this worthless damn hound." Well, Mom would just open the back door of the house, and in the dog would come like he owned the place. Yes sir, he just sat there next to Mom and ate everything she would pitch down onto the concrete floor for him, while Uncle Shorty gave him down the road. That dog knew where he was safe.

Old Jim loved to ride. He would go anywhere with anyone any time. You did not need to think about bringing him back, either. I can bet you that he had already been there more than once. So he knew if someone was going back; he would jump in their car or truck. Yes, he would. Everyone around just kind of tolerated him. Well, everyone, that is, except Shorty.

You see Old Jim did like his freedom. He would bark all night if you put him on a dog chain. He would dig without stopping, all the way to China if you put him in a pen. Jim just liked to sleep wherever he was. As for me, I admired that in him. He was right down independent.

Mamaw and Old Jim were buddies. She would never let on that she even liked the old dog. And, as I have stated many times, Old Jim did not like to run much. Even at mealtime he preferred that you carry food to him. On hot days, most dogs would just lay in the shade and pant with their tongues hanging out. Not Old Jim. He would go to the pond and take a quick dip and come to Grandmother's porch, where he would get as close to her rocking chair as he could. You see, Old Jim never saw his own mother; I brought him home when his eyes were still closed. The first people he ever saw were us. He truly never thought of himself as a dog. I think he looked upon himself as a perfect human forced to live with a bunch of two-legged dogs. That would be us.

Old Jim always used his smell as a way to separate himself from other humankind. One time he found a dead fish and rolled on it until he stunk so bad that I had to take him out in the river and wash him with a bar of lye soap. He liked to roll on dead road kill, fresh cow piles, rotten garbage — just about anything that would improve his aroma.

Mamaw walked with a cane. She had real bad arthritis and did not get around very well at all. Out on the front porch, she had one special rocking chair that she sat in every day. This was her fort for fighting gnats, flies, mosquitoes and an occasional honey bee. Mamaw was engaged in an ongoing war with houseflies. If her health had lasted another year or two, I think she alone could have placed "houseflies" on the endangered species list. She kept a small ring of dead flies around her at all times.

From her rocker, she could see the road and watch cars go by. Sometimes I thought she knew who was driving each one. She also observed happenings at Uncle Nelson's, so she made the correct reports to the rest of the family. And she kept up with who was coming and going at my house. She knew exactly what car was parked where, who was in it when it arrived and the exact time it departed and with whom. She did like her rocking chair, and so did Old Jim. I guess he was her one true confidant, kind of like the dog on the "Bushes Baked Beans" TV commercials. I have watched her have a whole conversation with Old Jim. She talked both sides of the conservation, while Old Jim just kind of slept some and watched her some.

One very hot day, Mamaw and me were setting on the porch talking. I had the porch swing moving back and forth just to have a little air movement. Old Jim was lying on his belly on concrete next to Grandmother. He just got up without saying a word or nothing. "Now where is he going?" Mamaw asked. (How do I know? I was thinking. I may have been the only one on the whole hill that thought Jim was a dog and could not speak one word of Appalachian American. I knew you couldn't talk to or even reason with him.) I answered back the best way I could, "Well, I don't know." In about five minutes Old Jim came back and lay down on the concrete beside Grandmother's rocker. He made a big wet spot. He had been to the pond to cool off.

When I took a bath I always tried to dab on some Old Spice. Well, I reckon Old Jim did the same. He had not been on the porch for more than a minute when Grandmother started to holler. I think Jim thought she was going into some kind of fit or something. She reared back with her cane and whopped Old Jim right on his head. He started to run like he had been set on fire. About this time the smell of rotten groundhog hit me. Grandmother was still screaming and almost running for the door. She almost didn't have arthritis. Aunt Maude came to see if she was dying.

I ran for the water bucket on the back porch and some smelly dish soap. I took to scrubbing the porch. Grandmother ran back to her room. She was going right slow, but for her she was running. Even now, I can still hear Old Jim as he went running past Mason Williams' Barber Shop and headed for Lovers Leap. He was barking his head off. The first time I saw this little ritual of theirs performed it kind of scared me some. But after the thousandth time, it just got to be funny. In less than an hour, Mamaw would be back at war with the flies, and Old Jim would be lying right close to her rocker.

Grandmother would be just rocking back and forth; Old Jim would have his tail going back and forth. Often his tail would be flipping under her rocker in perfect timing. Sooner or later, one of them would get out of rhythm, and he would get his tail mashed and be off running again. Sooner or later, one of the fresh-killed flies would land on Mamaw's foot, and Old Jim would lick it off. She would reward him with a whack on the head with her cane, and Jim would be off running and barking to the top of his lungs. Mamaw would set in her rocking chair and laugh so hard that her fat would shake. In about an hour, both Old Jim and Grandmother would be ready for round 236.

Every once in a while I got a call from the dog pound. Back then, Merrill Graham was the dog warden. I could hear his not-to-be-mistaken tone: "We done found Old Jim Dog again, and would you come and get him? He is eating the county out of house and pound." Once, Merrill delivered the dog back home to me. Old Jim was setting in the front of the dog pound truck. He was never made to ride in the back like a common dog. Sometimes you could see him swimming the river, so he could chase deer and rabbits in the Radford Arsenal. Then one morning, Old Jim up and went walk about and just never came back. He was a fine dog. I still miss Shorty and Old Jim.

The First Family Reunion

If I am not mistaken, the First Lytton Family Reunion was at the Prices Fork Fair Grounds in front of the old Grange Hall. It took place in 1965, or thereabout. Families came from everywhere. Some I knew, some I had heard of, but in some cases, I had no clue who these people were. I think I was about 12 or 13 years old and a true specimen of a young Appalachian Man. I probably owned a shirt or two, but I could not have told you where they were or the last time I had seen them and wasn't too prone to looking for them. Have you seen them? But anyway, I can bet that Momma had made me put on some kind of shirt. I can also bet that I did not like it! I did have short britches too, and I was truly tanned all over, and had no tan lines on me except for those around my ankles. You see, at this time I swam necked in New River except for a pair of old steel-toed, power plant work shoes. The sun felt good on my back, but the sharp rocks and ledges sometimes had their way with my feet. So I always wore the shoes.

I was skilled in the manly arts of chewing tobacco,

smoking cigarettes, smoking cigars and dipping snuff. I had a very good pipe, too. I did not have the good kind of snuff like Skoal and Copenhagen. I used the dry old Scotch Powdered kind. I learned that from Aunt Anna. When I wasn't coughing, I was sneezing from the snuff. I hated the stuff, but felt like I needed to learn how to like it. One time, I spit the juice from that Scotch Snuff on a tobacco worm, and the thing took to shaking all over and just fell off the tobacco plant dead! You know it was good stuff when you can kill a tobacco worm with one spit. I never tried the Copenhagen until I was much older. Chuck Shorter gave me some. Now, you talk about some coughing and shuddering.

Back to the reunion. I was also a good eater. Maybe I was the best in the whole family. After this fine meal we all agreed to go to the river swimming. We all loaded into Daddy's old blue Chevrolet, "Carry All." Literally, there was a head hanging out every window. In later stories, I called it a Suburban, to add a touch of class. We stopped at Grat's Store and picked up supplies for swimming. I got a couple packs of Chesterfield cigarettes, a plug of Apple chewing tobacco and a can of snuff. (Nope, I did not like the old powdered snuff, but I thought that I needed to show the new family members that I had some class and culture.) Finally we got to the river, and the second the car stopped, I shucked off most of my clothes and was in the water. I swam across the river like I had that old 1½ horse-power Elgin air-cooled outboard motor taped on my butt.

When I looked back at my newly discovered cousins,

they appeared to me to be looking for a hole to crawl in or an escape route. I do not think they were as happy to be on the river as I was. I don't think they were as impressed with me as I was. I don't think they had ever seen or been around a true Appalachian American like me before. In retrospect, I guess I should have been more willing to share my Apple Chewing Tobacco and Chesterfields. I do not think they would have wanted the powdered snuff; heck, I did not even want it. But, now, they did want to go home! I do not think that they have ever been back since. Possibly I should track them down and apologize.

The Full Benefit

Here is a short one, but a good one. Just hearing the words "full benefit" makes me think about my Uncle Shorty. Every once in a while, Shorty would load up all of the kids in the back of his pickup truck and take us to Tom Long's Store. Every one of us loved going to the store. We all liked riding in the back of the truck with wind blowing through our hair; it was fun. We also knew that we were going to get ice cream. Shorty would buy each of us a popsicle — any flavor you wanted. The only catch was you had to eat it as fast as you could. Only when your head started to hurt were you then getting the "Full Benefit" Uncle Shorty would say. I knew that pain was coming, but I ate it fast every time. There was not a mean bone in Shorty's body, except during hog killing. He just honestly liked seeing us get the full benefit from our popsicles.

You Know How Old Pickle Was

My daddy was pretty weak when it came to illness of any kind. One story Mom told had to do with when his tonsils became infected and had to be taken out, so he gave in at death's door and had the operation at the Old Christiansburg Hospital. When he went home after the surgery, nothing could make him comfortable. He would not eat or drink. He was not going to swallow for anything. It hurt far too much. Finally, he got so hungry that he paid Luther Snider to drive him back to the hospital and asked the doctor to give him "something to make the pain go away just long enough to eat." The doctor sprayed his throat with something. Elmer bolted from the office and ran across the street to a small diner and ate everything he could put his hands on before the numbing wore off. "Well, that will have to hold me until I heal up. Luther you can take me home now," he said.

On another occasion, I found a very large Corning beaker in the dump in Wake Forest (not the university, Wake Forest, in North Carolina; the Wake Forest near where we lived). I took the beaker home, set it up in the kitchen, and my brother Michael put a goldfish in it. It was so large that we had it sitting on an old car tire to keep it from turning over. Goldfish swam around in that thing for months. Then one day we all heard a quiet "ping." The sound was so quiet that we thought nothing of it. All of a sudden the floor was wet. I picked up the big beaker and ran for the door. When the thing broke in my hands, I received a major cut. We had to call Terry Albert to drive me to the emergency room at Radford Hospital. Daddy could not drive. He was too torn up at the thought of one of the kids being hurt. That was ok with me; you never knew when Daddy might have been in too bad a shape himself to drive.

When I was about three or four years old, I can remember falling out of the plum tree and my stomach hurting very badly. I faintly remember being in a hospital room with four or five older men and the strong smell of ether. But I cannot remember Daddy asking the doctor to put him to sleep for the surgery, too. As Mom tells it, Daddy told the doctor, "I am in as much pain as Charles and need to be put to sleep just to get through this."

The doctor said "No, we might need to ask you a question, and it would be best if only one baby is asleep at a time. So I want you to sit down and try to keep quiet." He did and Mom was holding my hand and rubbing me on the head when I went to sleep and still holding it when I woke up. My dear mother was just like that.

Uncle Shorty and the Demijohn

What is a demijohn? I sure did not know; as matter of fact, I had no clue what it was. Well, Uncle Shorty sure did know, and he put it to use, too. One of the tasks enjoyed by all solid, upstanding, redneck boys was going to the dump. I kid you not, I liked to go. We took trash to the dump real often. Sometimes we went to the dump just to see who else was dumping their trash. Sometimes we were digging through everybody else's trash. We were looking for overlooked treasures. Every once in a while, you would find one and haul it home, only to haul it back to the dump on the next trip.

Well, one warm smelly spring day, Shorty and me hauled the trash to the dump at Wake Forest. We are thinking that we will go to the dump and shoot a few rats and haul off the trash on the same trip. So we pitch out our trash. I reach for my gun, and before I can get my 22 loaded, Uncle Shorty walks over a few feet from the truck and says, "Hell, there is a demijohn." Now, I have no idea what he said or even what it meant. He may have sneezed or something. It could be a large striped snake or a giant new kind of rat for all I know. Both snakes and rats like the dump. It is neither. It is the biggest wine bottle I have ever seen.

A demijohn is a wine bottle that may hold two gallons or more. It is wrapped with wicker all around it. To me, it is exactly like a one-quart Italian Chianti wine bottle. You know, the ones you put candles in back in the seventies, and let candle wax run down over. I did not do this, for real rural folks would have laughed at me. But, in other houses I thought they were cool-looking. A demijohn was used somewhere in Europe for transporting wine. Maybe some water, too, but mostly wine, I think.

Shorty sets down on the tailgate of the truck holding this big bottle. He goes on to tell me that during World War II, he was in the navy and stationed in England. According to Shorty, everything but fog and air was rationed. You could not get anything at a store or through normal military channels. But if you had money and knew the man who knew another man, you could get about anything you wanted. "I mean anything!" says Uncle Shorty. The black market was alive and well on the English shores during World War II. He tells me of a lot of things he purchased, but did not bring home.

You may need to set down with Chuck to get caught up on this information; I blush too easy to write all the things down. But, Chuck doesn't blush that much. I do not know if I have told you this or not, but the Lyttons do like to take a little nip once in a while.

69

While in England, Shorty, and a few of his buddies put up the money for this big bottle of wine. In just a few days, the wine was delivered. It was in a great big reed-wrapped bottle, "a demijohn," Shorty goes on to say. "The wine was not any good wine like we make here at home; it was right strong and sour-like. Only a spaghetti bender would drink this stuff. But it did have alcohol in it. After a few drinks, it got to being ok, and in a little while it was good."

Shorty said that this one in the dump was only the second demijohn he had ever seen in this country. We took it home. He had no intention of setting the thing up and looking at it like a keepsake or an antique. He was going to put this bottle back into service. He washed it, and then washed it again. Remember, it came from the dump; a third washing would not hurt it one bit.

Shorty carried the jug to the meat house. There he set it with no less than ten one-gallon glass vinegar jugs. Over the next few hours, he collected up all the ingredients for a batch of home brew. As for me, I was trying very hard to remember the recipe, but I could not. I did remember a trip to the store to buy malt, yeast and sugar. Later that afternoon, in two very large earthen crocks, Shorty mixed the ingredients.

These are the same crocks that will be used for sauerkraut and pickles in a few months. Uncle Shorty poured the ingredients into the crocks, mixed it all up, and in less than a day the brew took on a real musty smell. Shorty said it was working. In a few more days it just stopped working, and we poured the stuff very carefully through a folded cheesecloth to filter out the dead yeast cells, old malt, bugs, flies, mud dabber bees and something Daddy and Nelson call the "The Mother." Damn, if it did not look like rough stuff!

We poured the home brew into the demijohn and all the other vinegar bottles and left the tops open with a piece of cheesecloth on top, just in case the stuff was still working some. After a few more days the brew had stopped working. Uncle Shorty again filtered it and now called the solution "henpeck." A little later, he capped each bottle. Since the big bottle did not have a bottle cap, we used a large fishing bobber made of cork. With care, Shorty fashioned a bottle stopper and pushed it down into the big bottle. The next morning we went to the cellar for a taste, but you could smell the place before we got there. Nelson and Daddy just said, "Oh no," when we opened the door. We were greeted by no less than one million fruit flies, bees and other bugs, some the size of hummingbirds. The homemade beer was still working. The home brew had exploded, and the mess was everywhere. I mean home brew was on the floor, the walls and on the jars of food. But the big wine bottle was still there.

Rather than break, the old bottle shot the cork out the top. Rather than start cleaning up the glass and mopping up the floor, Shorty, Nelson and Daddy set down on the little bench in the cellar and started drinking the home brew from the big bottle. Now the stuff was still working, but they didn't care. They were not going to take any chances that this bottle might break, too. I do not remember them getting more than a little tipsy, but they got real sick. They all had a bad dose of "backdoor trots," as Grandmother called it.

Where the old bottle went, I had no clue. In fact I had not given the big bottle one thought in 50 years or more until the fall of 2009, when I took the urge to go squirrel hunting. Not sure where to go, I took a walk through the woods just below the old hog pen, the place where I went as a kid. Kevan had driven a bulldozer just below Uncle Shorty's garden and just above the old rusty car. There isn't much left of the old rusty car. Mother Earth has just about reclaimed it. Well anyway, Kevan had made a real nice path to walk on and to hunt from.

Like in the past, I set down on the edge of the holler. There are no squirrel cuttings; in fact, there are no nut trees either. It doesn't matter; this is the spot where I used to set. I scratch around to make myself comfortable in the cool breeze that blows up the holler off the river, and the rustle of tree leaves makes me think of my youthful days setting right here. One of the things that I find is a large piece of curved brown glass. I know by its shape that it came from Uncle Shorty's old big demijohn bottle. On the spot, I stop thinking about squirrels and start remembering Uncle Shorty's stories of the first demijohn bottle he saw many years ago in England. I think of him hooking up shore electrical current to his big ship. I start remembering a very funny story about cooking on the wharf where the ship was moored and drinking the sour wine from a big brown glass bottle. I also remember the other stories, too. I find it funny how an old piece of broken brown glass can hold so many good memories.

I have no idea when the old bottle was broken. I wonder how Kevan did not cover it up when he made the road. Why is this one big piece left? Then it dawns on me. Uncle Shorty just wanted me to tell this story, so we could remember the trip to the dump and his treasure. I do remember, and I pitch that piece on down over the hill toward the old rusty car. This is where it ort to be anyway. Just let history have it I think. I think I will do the remembering for you, Uncle Shorty!

The Ladies' Church Meeting

Daddy was a fifth grade graduate of Long Shop Elementary. (In his words, "I attended LSU.") I never did get to go to the old school in Long Shop, and I wish I had. The old school was a very simple, square two-story clapboard building. There was a water pump in front and two outhouse toilets in the back. Each room had a coal stove. Outside there was a big ballfield. There were no snow days, either. The only reason to miss school was you were sick, I mean real sick. If it rained or snowed, you went to school.

Uncle Shorty was nicknamed "Shorty," because he was real small for his age. Miss Lottie Smith made it her business to watch all the kids walking up the Sucker Snider Hill on their way home. She lived right at the crest. According to her, it had been snowing and drifting all day, and there was a big drift in the curve beside her house. She knew that she had seen four Lytton kids and Jake Lovern when they topped the hill. Now she counted only four; one was missing. She waited a few more minutes, and when the fifth kid did not appear she went looking. Not far from her house she found Shorty pinned against the barbed wire fence by the wind and snow. He just could not get himself loose. Mamaw said that Miss Lottie said, "He was about give out and was screaming and cussing with every breath." She took him into the house and warmed him up and sent him on his way.

I always like that story; I do think it is true. Shorty, too, said that it happened, but each time Miss Lottie told it, the wind was a little harder and the snow got deeper and the barbed wire was newer. "I was damn near give out, and I was cold," Shorty would say. The saddest part of this story is that I missed all the good things. I missed the deep snow, wind and knowing that there was someone to drag you out of the snowdrift. That darn Al Gore. Why in the world did he have to go ruin things by inventing global warming?

About every time Daddy, Shorty, Nelson and Mod Snider got together to share a good drink of whatever licker they had, they'd lapse back into stories about each other and the shenanigans they did. Shorty and Daddy loved to tell the story about when it was time for Grandmother to host the monthly Ladies' Church Meeting.

The hostess always made a big bowl of fruit punch. Mamaw made a special punch, and everyone always liked it. She poured a quart or two of canned grape juice, canned apple juice, some berry juice and about any other fresh fruit juice she had into a bowl. She set the punch bowl in the cellar to cool down. Just before the ladies were to show up, she would chip off some clean ice and put it in the bowl. Everyone on the hill just loved cold fruit punch.

Grandmother sent Nelson and Shorty to the cellar for the punch while Uncle Lake chipped off small pieces of ice from the big blocks in the ice house. Grandmother tasted her creation, and it was just about as good as it could get. When the first lady came, Grandmother showed her to the punch, and she got herself one of them little cups full. Old women do not like to take big drinks or have large coffee cups of punch. After the other ladies filed in, Grandmother asked one of the aunts to fill the punch bowl back up. While she did so, Shorty poured a quart of moonshine in the punch bowl.

The crowd of young people, boys and girls alike, just sat around and watched as the conversation got louder, and the old women started talking about the shortcomings of the husbands and other men friends. Daddy said, "If you want to know just anything about anybody, get two of the most strictest and stern old spinsters about half drunk, and you can learn a lot of unspoken and untold secrets — secrets that you should not know. A lot of people learned about the birds and the bees listening over a bowl of punch."

Every time the group met, it did not matter at whose house, an extra crowd was there to add the moonshine and learn more about humor, how to deal with life's situations and another lesson on the birds and the bees. At school, Shorty said: "For a few days after one of the 'Hen Sessions,' boys and girls picked at one another, laughing at things that their grandmothers had said about activities they had allegedly engaged in their youth."

"Every once in a while, you just might be surprised to learn who your daddy truly was," said Daddy.

One of the Worst Jobs
There Ever Was

Now my father, Elmer, was truly one of the good old boys. He would give you the shirt off his back. He never ever missed one day of work until he was laid up with Degenerative Rheumatoid Arthritis. Once the arthritis took a hold of him, he never was much good after that. Also, as I said in some other story, Elmer was a sexist son of bitch. But the worst job is not about Elmer. It involves my mother Ruth.

Ruth never learned to drive until much later in her life. She started learning when she was about 50 years old. In fact, I am now saddened to say, I learned to drive years before she did. Sometimes, when I was right young, Mom would take us all to town shopping during the week, but the Old Cream Bus had stopped running. She sure was old enough to drive, but she didn't. On these days a young man or older boy would come over the hill to our house.

I can remember him coming into the house, walking in,

and saying, "Hey, Elmer said that you needed to go to town and he gave me a dollar and car keys to drive you." Back then you did not knock. I think the host would have thought that you were being uppity or trying to put on airs if you knocked.

I also think that this embarrassed Mom, having to explain her business to this 16- or 17-year-old boy. Plus she had to feed the sorry rascal. Well, it wasn't his fault. Mom would then load us into the car, and sometimes she would have to go and get Grandmother, too. Off to town we would go. We would buy groceries, go to the Leggett store, sometimes even buy hog feed. The driver would not even help load the stuff in the car. "Harmie, I ain't paid to do no heavy liftin' or carryin'. You are big for your age; you go on now and help your mother." Since he was calling me Harmie, a name that changed once I entered first grade, I could not have been six years old. Now this bossiness business used to boil the oil in me, but you just had to go on and do it.

I can tell you a 100-pound sack of hog chop was heavy for an 80- or 90-pound boy. At home I had a wheelbarrow to move feed, but not here. At the feed store I also observed if a grown man came, the owner would help him load his feed. He just never came to help Momma and me. Somehow we got it in the car.

I can remember, after about each one of these trips out into the world, Mom would say to Daddy, "Just why can't you teach me how to drive? That way I can come and go as I need and want to." Elmer never said much back. That meant, "No."

I think that in his sexist way he wanted Mom to stay right on River Ridge and under his thumb and control.

Well, as I got older, I drove about everything there was on the hill. Me and Elmer would slip off, and he would drink himself a beer while I sat on his lap steering the car down the road. When I was little, I would help out on the farm. My legs were too short to reach the brakes and clutch, but I could steer the truck while bigger boys picked up hay. They would set a pop crate in the seat to boost me up so I could see over the hood, then pull out the manual throttle and set me a slow speed across the field. I had a great time, all the while just dreading when I had to start pitching the hay bales and yield my pop crate to some other little boy. All true, red-blooded Appalachian American Boys did this. We all knew how to drive by the time we could see over the hood.

Elmer said to me one day, "Someday you will be old enough to drive your mother and grandmother to town to do business." I never gave one thought about this. That was just the way I was raised. When I was in the tenth grade in high school, I chipped a bone in my shin. It swelled up about the size of a cocoanut. I had go to the doctor, and Mom had to go too because she knew about the family insurance and other stuff. So I had to drive to Radford Hospital; Mom was the passenger. After the outpatient surgery I had to again drive home. Mom could not drive. Two weeks later, I drove back to Radford Hospital. Mom still could not drive; she could only ride.

Girls did not drive, and Mom was a girl, so in our house she did not learn to drive. This rule held true for all the Lytton women living on the hill. Aunt Tootie, Aunt Maude and my mother could not drive. One day I could legally do so. I went about everywhere, and never gave one thought to the fact that neither Mom nor my older sister could drive.

Finally one day, Mom asked me to teach her to drive. It dawned on me that the world of driving education was upside down. By all that was right, she ought to be teaching me! Now this was one hell of an experience; one that few on River Ridge ever forgot. We had a VW bus; yes, one of those that looked like a "Hippie Bus." I did with Mom just like Dad had done with me: we went to the farm at Whitethorne. I drove out on one of the big fields where there was nothing to hit. Mom knew about gears, breaks, the clutch and steering. She said she had been practicing in her mind for a long time. The only problem was she had never tried to do any of these things.

Well, Dear Old Mom gets behind the wheel with all of her pride and knowledge, and she cannot start the thing. After awhile she had starting down pat, but going was another matter. The way she let out the clutch, that poor old VW jumped all over the field before she got the thing going. First she went too fast, then too slow. And going and shifting gears was a whole different matter. You get the picture. She was trying to put 30 years of watching into action in one day. "Why in the blank, blank hell won't it go?" she would yell. I was so nervous I was thinking about taking up drinking, and I do not mean Pepsi either.

One of the best driving experiences was the time Mom ran the VW over the hill toward the pond. She was practicing her clutching, and the VW got away from her. When I came home, the VW was missing, and there set Mom just looking at me. She pointed down over the hill toward the pond, and there set the VW. I knew exactly what to do, since I had run the thing over the hill a year earlier while I was practicing my clutching in the driveway. We just drove it back up over the hill, and no one was the wiser except me and Mom. And a few hundred close friends. We now knew to keep an eye out for the bank heading toward the pond.

There was a young lady who lived right up the road from us and knew our family well. She was aware of Mom's driving skill and her wish to drive. Every afternoon she and Mom took a ride and in no time Mom was driving as good as anyone on the road. She came and went as she wished. Me, I was so proud of her!

What I think is funny here is Elmer became disabled and could not drive a lick. Mom had to play chauffeur and haul him all around the country. Dad would say, "Your mother, she is a good driver." I guess that all is well that ends well. But it did embarrass me to be the one who had to start teaching his own mother to drive.

Elmer's Old Ukulele

Uncle Shorty once said to me, blood and family is a tight bind! It makes no difference if-n they are good or bad, they are yours.

I reckon that it is the summer of 1958. I ain't very old, but I am sure enough old enough to know better and that is fact! There is a group of people setting around in our front yard. I listen to them talk and rehash old stories about the Depression, World War II, the weather and gardens. After a little while, I am bored stiff, so I go back into the house.

There isn't anyone in the house, so I go to looking through stuff that I shouldn't and in places where I am not permitted to be. Back in the bottom of the old chiffonier closet, I find a little guitar, actually an old wooden ukulele. The strings are loose, and it will not make much of a sound. When I go to tighten up the strings, I twist the little tighteners so hard that one of the strings breaks. So I move on to the next string, and it snaps too. I start on the third string. It does not break, but the little wooden thing that holds the string pops off.

I look around for a few seconds and then slip out through the back door. I get to thinking that I should fix the ukulele before anyone knows what I have done. I go down to the old building next to the hog lot. I put the ukulele up on the workbench and look the situation over. I figure the best thing for me to do is find some really small nails and nail the string holder back onto the ukulele. I am just trying get the nail started when both the string holder and ukulele split. My nail is sticking in big crack in the ukulele.

I do not know what to do or what to say. I just stand there looking like a still-born calf. All of a sudden, the door to the building opens and in steps Mr. Franklin Littleton. He is always the nicest man. In one step, he is standing beside me. "Where did you get this, and do you have any idea what you have done? This here is the ukulele your daddy carried all over the South Pacific during World War II and tried to play and sing to your Mama. If he don't bust your little ass, I am going to!"

Mr. Littleton took me and the ukulele home. I told my story to Daddy, and he just looked at me. "You know that when you break something that ain't yourn, you ort to go and tell the person you broke it. All it would have taken is a walk over to Mr. Luther's to have him glue the string holder back on. Can't do that now, can you?" He just looked at me. For once, Elmer did not holler or cuss. He just looked at me. Nothing more needed to be said!

I did learn to keep myself out of other people's stuff and to be real careful with other people's things. I never ever saw the ukulele ever again. Nothing was said to me about it ever again. Mr. Littleton never said another word. In a while, I forgot about it. But every once in while I chuckle thinking about Elmer trying to sing to Momma. I just guess there was a time when they both were younger; they must have been a whole lot younger. Maybe, that is why the ukulele was in the bottom of the closet.

The Shock of a Lifetime!

Elmer once told me that it is sometimes harder to be a man who is in the right than to drift by in the wrong. I think what he meant is, it is sometimes hard to stand up when you are right.

One time, Elmer and me had a part-time job. After I outgrew well-drilling, we went to work cleaning and maintaining telephone booths. Every Saturday and Sunday, this job took us all over the county. Again, the main focus was to keep my mind occupied and my body busy. Daddy did not care one whit what I was doing, as long as I was busy. At the time, there were telephone booths all over this county. We would just pull up in the parking lot in front of the telephone booth, and I'd wash each window, check the light bulbs and make minor repairs.

This one day we show up at the Marina Bridge, on the shore of Claytor Lake. There is a big box and a bunch of aluminum pieces in a pile. I get to looking around and see there is also a little square concrete pad with an electrical wire sticking out of it. I learn that we are going to make a telephone booth. It isn't hard. I empty out the box and start putting the pieces together like a big aluminum puzzle. Within two hours I am standing up on the top of the newly assembled telephone booth, mounting the telephone sign.

Now, Elmer decides not to take a real active part. Up to this point he has been inside drinking coffee, looking at boats, and other things. He wants to see if the electricity has been turned on. He goes into the building and flips the breaker. Please keep in mind that I am standing on top of the booth mounting the light fixture when Pap turns on the power. I am shocked so bad that I fall off.

My whole body is hurting and just trembling and I'm a-screaming. Everyone from the store, marina and parking lot comes running to my aid. Some might have swum from across the lake. About this time, Daddy comes out of the basement and starts hollering at me, "The very first minute I turn my back, you quit on me. You know, I can't take my eyes off of you. I will never get this job done if you keep goofing off and setting there on the ground. We got work to do."

My small crowd of concerned people just slowly walks away and says not one word. In a minute or two, I stop twitching and jerking. The screams have stopped, and I am back to kind of mumbling in an unknown language. So I just climb back up on top of the telephone booth; but only after I go into the basement and put the electrical fuses in my pocket. Elmer goes back to drinking coffee and looking around.

Some things never change. I also went to the bathroom

to check my britches. They were a little streaked, but nothing more than normal. I had not soiled them; just why I cannot figure out. The shock should have jolted the crap out of me. The fall could have knocked the stuffings out of me. Somehow I just held on to both!

My First Trip to the Doctor

Miss Hattie Guynn, my fourth grade teacher, once told me: "You have far too much curiosity, and one day all that curiosity is going to come home and bite you. You just wait and see."

To be honest I do not actually remember all of the details of this day as well as my Mom does or did. You see, I was only five years old at the time. Mom likes for everyone to know about this. She has told this story to everyone she ever met. Miss Jocelyn May had a few laughs at my expense over this, too. She was the nurse in the doctor's office and saw it all start to finish. She always told this story at the little church beside Mr. Galimore's Store. It all started when I got a new pair of undershorts.

Now, if you hear this phrase from your mom and daddy, take off running: "Put on your new pair of undershorts. You never know when you might be in a car wreck, and you don't want the doctor at the hospital to think you don't have any." You see, at the time of the story I was truly house-broken and could find my own way to the toilet. But I wasn't broke to wearing underwear yet. It was just that I could not get the knack for them rascals; they itched and they were tight. They kind of bound me up.

It was the summer of 1956. I ought to be able to tell you the day and minute of my first trip to the doctor, but I can't. I do know that it was late summer, because all of the apple trees were in full leaf and had lots of hard, green, sour apples on them. Possibly I have a mental block against that date or something. Humor me for a sentence or two. I was five years old and right big for my age. I entered the first grade weighing 46 pounds and was almost 40 inches tall. I had lots of older cousins. They were nice enough to give me all of their old clothes: shoes, socks, undershorts — 'bout everything. Some fit, some had holes and some had other things too.

At this phase of my life I probably didn't even know that you could get new clothes. They just came in a bag from your bigger cousins. I bet Arnold, Lynwood, Ronnie and Myron had even bigger cousins, so there might have been some history I didn't figure on. When aunts and cousins came with clothes, I was stripped down about naked to stand on the kitchen table at Grandmother's house. Everything of much importance started at Grandmother's house. Over the next few minutes, they brought in clothes and made you put them on. There were shirts, pants and underwear. Each aunt just took turns putting stuff on you. If it fit, it was now yours. I was right rough on stuff like clothes, so no one ever came looking for my hand-me-downs.

One morning, while I was setting in the top of the big

white oak tree in the backyard, Aunt Letty came to visit. From my lofty perch I watched her first go to Grandmother's. Then I saw her coming up over the hill with a bag. She and Mother gave out a holler: "Harmie, get down out of that tree and come here." "Harmie," that was me back then. I jumped out of the tree and came running. You never knew what was in the bag. It might have been a cake or something; you just never knew.

This time it was for sure not a cake. It was pants, not just a regular pair of pants. They were dress pants! The kind grown people only wore in town. Sometimes you might see an old man with a pair of them britches at church, but not often.

I was made to stand in the middle of the table to try them on. Holy Moly! They itched. They were 100% wool. Within a minute, I was very hot and itched so much that I could not stand still to see how much alteration they needed. These pants would best be worn to the pond in the dead of winter to chop a hole in the ice for the cows and horses to drink through. They were not for summer wear at all, but here they were on me.

"They are a little big," said Aunt Letty, "but he is big for his age, you know." The sad part is I did fill them out. I thought they needed to be cut off at about the knees or just under the pockets to let some air in.

"A little taking up in the waist will help," Mom said. Then they went to sewing, and left me standing on the kitchen table with my brand new hand-me-down underwear on.

91

In just a few minutes, the sewing was completed, and I tried them on a second time. Them old hand-me-down britches fit like a charm. The legs were good. The butt was fine, but the waist came up real high on my ribs. The bottom of the zipper was right at my navel; the button latched right in the middle of my chest, just over my nipples. "Heavens, them are special pants for some big and important things. You could tell because the belt come up real high on your chest. I sure wish I had some of them too," said Daddy. Heck, you almost did not need a shirt with them things on. With a little hitch up, you could have cut armholes in them and wore them like my bibbed overalls.

Early one morning, most likely a Saturday, I was caught up and put in a 30-gallon galvanized bathtub in the basement. Treatment like this was reserved only for Saturday night and never early on a Saturday morning. Something was going on here, for sure! After I got dried off, I saw those hot itchy pants, a clean button-up shirt and a pair of brand new white, never-ever-been-worn underpants. I was not made to wear underwear except when we went toward town, and I had never had a pair of new ones before.

At this point, I knew what was coming. It was my first trip to the doctor, or rather the first one I can remember in any detail. I had been once before for a hernia operation. I do not remember much about that except the bad taste of ether and being locked up in large room with five or six sick men and Mom sitting by me holding my hand and rubbing my fuzzy short hair before surgery. After surgery she was still setting there by me rubbing my short stubby hair. "Everything is going to be all right. You wait and see," she was saying. I think she was crying some, too. Mothers are like that, you know. But this Saturday morning was something altogether different.

Well, with this old hospital memory running through my mind, I took to running and I mean fast, hard and far. Mom and Dad were out in the yard hollering for me, but there was no way they could find me right up in the very top of the biggest apple tree in the orchard. Daddy drove the car over. He hollered out the window for me to climb down "Get in. You are going to the doctor. I don't like it much either, but you got to go. It's the law, so get in," Daddy said. I got in, and they took me.

We went to see Doctor Johnson. Mom took me in, because Daddy just could not go. He was afraid of doctors, so he just set in the car and waited for us. In fact, all the way to town I had heard my parents discussing how much of a baby Daddy was and the pain he had experienced. I figured that was what they call "man pain," and I was fixing to learn a lot about some "boy pain." All of this made it really hard to relax. I just kind of wanted to soil my brand new undershorts, but somehow I held on and didn't.

Mom took me in; I mean "she took me in." Miss Jocelyn May put us in a room that smelled really bad, but the smell was the least of my worries. It was no wonder that Poor Elmer was so scared of the doctor. There were glass shelves all around the room. There were needles and syringes on each shelf. Some of the needles were curved, some were long, and some were very large. Some of them surely could have been used on horses. Heck, Dr. Johnson might be a damn veterinarian or something. I was thinking that they have done brought me to a horse doctor. No human, not even one big for his age, could stand a needle like those. And someone was getting very scared.

Dr. Johnson talked with Mom and said very little to me. Once in while he would cut his eyes toward me and work his head up and down. Miss Jocelyn came into the room carrying a big syringe on a little metal serving tray with a paper napkin on it. I was going to get a shot. She told me to take down them high britches and bend over on the table, and I did. The room smelled bad, the plastic on the table was cold as ice and my butt was sticking right up in the cold air. I could feel the chill bumps running up and down my butt; some chill bumps were going crossways, too. I took to shaking like a cold wet dog trying to pass a peach seed. "Now, you hold still," she told me. She washed a little spot on my butt with some alcohol. I was shaking so bad that I did not think she could hit that little alcohol covered target the way my butt was shaking! I knew it was the place she was aiming that needle; I knew what was coming.

About the time Miss Jocelyn launched that needle toward my rear end, I drew up my butt muscles real tight and hard. My butt is harder than Chinese arithmetic, and we both know that is the hardest kind of arithmetic there is. When that needle hit my butt, it went in funny; it bent. Mom let out an

"Ooohhh" sound. I let out a low-pitched scream, the kind of scream an elephant does that can be heard for 15 or 20 miles. Miss Jocelyn let out a squeal for Dr. Johnson. I later asked Uncle Shorty if he heard me scream, and he said that he did not. But then again he had been down at the coal mine and truly my screams might not have got there yet.

Dr. Johnson rushed into the room and quickly looked things over. He then told me to "relax, this may sting." That is short for: "You are going to think you have been stung by a large bunch of yellow-jackets right on your ass." Miss Jocelyn came back with a second needle, and it wasn't on a serving tray this time. He pulled the bent needle out, and while I was still in the screaming mode he gouged a new needle in my butt. He painted on some Merthiolate and put a big piece of white tape about the size of large piece of popcorn on the site of the bent needle. I am fine now, 55 years later. It is over, and I ain't ever needed to go back. No, never again.

As Mom related the story to Daddy, he looked like he was going to be really sick. "I told you that I cannot take going to the doctor, didn't I?" Elmer said. Then he got really quiet and white looking; I thought that he was going to run the car into the ditch along the road. To this day, I have a little gristle in my butt where Dr. Johnson pulled the needle out. Boys and girls, you have got to know this. When someone pulls out a brand new pair of undershorts for you, beware. They might be taking you to the doctor.

Smoking in the Tree

When I was no more than 13 years old, my father gave me this piece of advice. "Don't always be bumming cigarettes from Nelson and Shorty. If you are going to smoke, go to work and buy your own." If you want something out of this world you have got to go to work!

I could always get cigarettes from Uncle Nelson and Shorty. "Now take them cigarettes and go to the bluff, climb a tree somewhere and smoke them up," they would tell me. "Them limbs and leaves will break up the smoke and no one can see it." I know it works, because I have set up there in the sky so close and with wind just whipping through my fuzzy hair. Unknown to the world, I set there just smoking away on my short Chesterfields!

In the summer months, the best place for smoking was in the apple trees out in the little meadow between Nelson's and Shorty's houses. I loved to set up in small limbs of those trees and gnaw on hard green apples covered with a thin layer of salt and smoke away on my cigarettes. I liked to look down over May's Holler. I could see the horses and cows graze and even see rabbits and birds. The birds just loved to come to the newly burned ash piles and roll and flop like they were taking a bath or something. I was always on the lookout for airplanes coming over. I was bothered wondering where the stuff went if someone went to the bathroom on an airplane, and I did not want my suspicions to come true.

The best cigarettes for airplane-watching and just seeing the world keep on turning were Chesterfield, Lucky Strike and Pall Mall — all unfiltered. Why? Because that is what Uncle Nelson and Shorty smoked. They were strong and made me cough like a real big plot hound hot on a fresh bear track in the deep woods! I just never could get used to that coughing or that deep down in the lung wheeze them unfiltered cigarettes gave me. I figured someday, when I was older, I would smoke them filtered Winstons. I knew I liked them, because Uncle Lake would give them to me when he visited. I also knew those good days would just have to wait until I could land myself a paying job. So I just kept on smoking and a-hacking.

Here is one funny little story about Uncle Lake and smoking. When Lake came to River Ridge to visit, he smoked and drank just like my dad and my other uncles. When Aunt Nelly came with him, Uncle Lake slipped around just me to smoke and snitch a little nip. He was just scared of Aunt Nelly, and I think she kept him on a right short leash. At least that is what Daddy always said. We were out behind the big two-hole toilet at Grandmother's just smoking away when out of the corner of Lake's eye he saw Aunt Nelly walking toward us. Lake just stuck the Winstons in the pocket of my shorts and started into some long past story. "You should not be encouraging that boy to begin the smoking habit," Aunt Nelly said. I thought that I had it bad, having to slip around and smoke. Heck, Uncle Lake was a grown man, and he still was slipping around.

But life was good — a good cigarette, blue sky, a good sour apple covered with salt and a fine breeze. I was truly hidden from the world, or so I thought. The only people that knew where I was and what I was doing were Nelson, Shorty, Toot, Grandmother, Mom, Daddy, Gilbert Hilton and Mason Williams, Luther and Mamie Snider, Miss Helen, Mr. Walker, Aunt Beedie, and Sam Smith and. . . heck, everybody knew! I was the only one fooled by my smoking. I guess I was about ten when one day Daddy told me to "stop bumming cigarettes from people and start buying your own." He gave me a full brand new pack of L&M Cigarettes, the filtered kind, and said: "The next pack you got to buy. So find some work!"

Now, I did keep on smoking, but it never was as much fun after that. Soon I never climbed a tree to hide and I almost never smoked again. Life is sure funny. Today sometimes I will fire up my old pipe and smoke it regular for a week or so. I reckon Old Elmer knew me better than I knew myself. Be careful what you wish for, since you just might get it and it won't be any good anymore.

There once was a big red oak tree on the farm at Whitethorne. It stood on the big hill back toward McCoy. It was a very big and easy to climb. For some reason, people working on the farm seemed to gather near this old tree. I think it was because the shade was the coolest around, and the peace and quiet was something to only whisper about. It was so high I thought I could see all the way to Blacksburg from the top. Up there I would set and smoke and drink an occasional free beer. Boys just need places like this!

When I was about 12 or 13 years old the old farm was sold. The first thing the new owners did was to start logging, and one of the first trees cut was the old big red oak. Not in my lifetime would I ever climb another tree like it. "Well I reckon you won't be climbing that tree anymore," said Uncle Nelson as we sat by the mailbox and watched a load of logs pass. "I think that I saw your big log go past today." Time does march on.

A Fast Ride on Something Without Wheels

When I would ask for something, I always found it funny when Elmer would answer, "Crap in one of your hands and hold the other out for money and see which one fills first."

In or around 1960 or 1961 it started snowing in early December and did not let up until the last of January. That year I think we missed more than 30 days of school. When things got straightened out, we went to school on Saturdays too. Damn if that wasn't a change! I wasn't too crazy about school anyway, and I just hated Saturday School. Mom made me go, but there weren't more than three or four other kids there. Most of the teachers even laid out, too. Oh no, not me; I was there. The other kids all caught the 24-hour mumps or whooping cough or something, but they were okay on Monday.

Finally, the weather had started to warm up a little during the day, and the snow melted some. It was still getting very cold at night. The remaining snow had formed a very thick, hard, icy crust. I could walk on the top of the snow crust in the mornings.

One morning, like usual, I am down at Uncle Nelson's to help him feed the hogs. The deal is if I carry the slop bucket, all the water for the chop, and three or four five-gallon buckets of water from the pond for the hogs, he will roll me a few Prince Albert cigarettes.

In the winter, hogs could drink lots of water, so I made a lot of trips to the spigot or the pond. I want you to know that I do know how to roll my own cigarettes, but Nelson told me I was too wasteful. So he did it for me.

This particular morning, Uncle Nelson launched into a story about sleigh-riding when he was a boy. He told me about a time when he went off the hill behind us in a wooden orange crate. [I am talking about the flat place near Nelson and Tootie's house along the main road. There once was a hill there, but the county hauled it off to Prices Fork for a road improvement project. It took about a month, but they took and moved that hill.] Nelson said he went down the hill very fast. The orange crate got up on top of the crust and just went. "Hell of a ride" he said. Water ran out of both of his eyes and went right up into his hair he was going so fast.

When we finished smoking up our cigarettes, and I had carried the buckets back to the house, Nelson's last words were always the same: "Don't tell anyone I gave you cigarettes, and for God's sake don't tell Ruth." I often wonder why Mom never said anything about smoking cigarettes. I know to my soul she could smell them. I guess it was because about everybody smelled of cigarettes.

Well, I thought about how much fun that sled ride would be, and I started looking everywhere for a wooden box. I was playing in Shorty's barn when I found an old wooden dynamite box. It was probably left over from when they worked the mines in McCoy. I carefully dumped its contents into a very neat pile and headed for the road. There stood Nelson at the mailbox counting passing cars. To his dying days, Nelson liked to watch cars go by. As I started off around the hardtop to the pond on top of the hill, Wooster shuffled down over the hill to check his hogs.

Right near the pond on the hilltop, I pitched the dynamite box over the fence and crawled under the barbed wire after it. I carried it over to the knoll at the top of the hill. With my bare hands, I held onto a limb of the big cedar tree as I got in the thing and pushed off. Boy oh boy! I already wished that I had had on some gloves. The whole ride could not have lasted more than 30 or 40 seconds, but it felt like an hour.

Within a second, I felt like I was riding on a rocket! I could see Nelson over at the hog lot, and he was laughing, just hooting and hollering. Me, I was just holding on for my life. I should have taken to crying, but there was not time. The snow had melted down to the point that flint rocks were just barely covered with snow and ice. That wooden box did not miss one. I would hit one, and the box would change direction. Sometimes I was pointed toward the river. Other times I was pointed back toward the hilltop. Hit another rock, and I would lurch around and change direction again. Like Daddy would say, I was "spinning around like the button on an outhouse door." Yes, I hit many rocks and rode down a lot of smaller catalpa and black locust trees, but the thick blackberry patches were just awful.

How I missed the large trees and the barbed wire fence around the potato patch is a mystery to me. I never gave a thought to the old cistern at Great Grandmother Adalie's burnt house. Now that would have been something to have discovered on this ride. Down through the holler I went, totally out of control. I knew if I jumped out of the box, one of the little trees might cut off my head all the way back to my shoulders or something. I knocked over rocks, limbs and old blocks of wood and still I came on.

Then it was over, and I was mostly alive. I hit the railroad gate. Fortunately it was one of those heavy metal ones. It sounded like the train wreck of Old 97. I just laid there on the ice and snow for a few minutes and then somehow sat up. A minute or two later, I got up. I wasn't broken anywhere. But there wasn't a place that wasn't hurting. I was bruised up a lot from hitting the gate. The wooden box was broken. The most hurt part of me was my hands and fingers. The trees and blackberry briars had been kind of rough on them. My knuckles were as pale as a ghost and were hurt and cramping from holding on. I had been holding as tight as one holds on in a dentist chair. Some of those knuckles had blood dripping off of them.

I went to Mamaw's house. When I told her what I had

done, she just looked at me shaking her head and kind of hissing through her teeth. "Are you okay? You know you are crazy and dumb as that Nelson? Don't you know you could have been killed or worse? Also, you have got to stop listening to people telling you these wild stories. But, keep in mind, you faired better than Nelson. Did your Uncle Nelson tell you about his ride over the hill? Did he tell you that I had to go help him back up to the house? You see, he broke his arm."

The son-of-a-bitch did not tell me that my boyish eagerness was going to get me killed. I do wish that Uncle Nelson had given me a little warning. It most likely would not have stopped me, but I might have found me a pair of gloves. I told him, "The next time we are feeding the hogs and smoking cigarettes, I am not going to listen to your stories, and I want some filtered Winstons, too." I said to myself, I will filter his stories through this experience. For a while, he still rolled me few of those rotten Half and Half tobacco things he smoked. At 7 or 8 years old you cannot be too picky about your cigarettes.

Off to the Barn Loft

I once asked if I could do something or another, and Mother answered back, "Once you get all of the question figured out, most likely the correct answer will be waiting there for you." Yes or no was out of the question.

In the late summer, when real big thunderheads would build up over the mountains in the direction of McCoy and a little cool breeze blew toward River Ridge, the air would be thick and temperatures very hot. Soon the sweet summer rains would start to fall with every clap of thunder. "Sweet summer rains" is what Grandmother called summer thunderstorms. About this time most all of our family would go to the barn loft and take a nap.

Daddy liked the sound of the rain on the tin roof and the cool air that swept through the big door on the river side of the barn. I think he liked all of us kids piled up about him, too. Mom just needed us to be out of the house for a few hours. We were starting to get on her nerves or something. The house was small. "You all are getting right close in on me," she would say.

The hillside was almost free of trees back then. I have set in the barn and watched big storms come up the river from way down below Cowan Siding. Sometimes only a few drops fell on the barn's roof, while people fishing on the river were caught in a deluge. Often the rainbow looked like it was just outside the barn. "See God even likes to come to the barn on hot rainy afternoons. Can't beat that sweet summer rain," Elmer would say, as he looked out over the big hillside garden.

I would simply pile up a few empty feed sacks on the hay and set back and enjoy the cool draft coming through the barn. Off to sleep I would go. Sometimes I would wake up, and the cool air of night would be on me and it would be pitch dark outside. Once in a while, I would not wake up until Uncle Shorty came in the early morning to milk.

There might be two or three old dogs and a cat or two on the sacks with me. Maxine, our collie dog, was always right up against my back. I think she liked me. Daddy and the others just left me asleep. I guess the rain on the tin roof worked. I would stumble out of the loft and head for home. I did not mind walking home in the dark. But I did mind them dog fleas that always got on me and the small scratches from the course hay. Every stray dog and cat for miles around slept in the barn, too. They kept the place infested with fleas, ticks and dog mange. I don't think that I caught the mange, but I often did catch the fleas. When that happened, Momma would wash me with real hot water and lots of lye soap. The fleas just can't stand lye soap. She would also set down on a chair by me with a pair of tweezers and a needle and pull the ticks off me.

Back in the late 1950s and early 1960s, satellites and space rockets were a new thing. On real hot summer nights, we would strip down about naked and lie outside on the dew-dampened grass in the cool night air and watch for satellites. We did this for hours on end. It was just too hot to go inside the little cinderblock house. Mom kept a stack of old half-worn-out quilts and blankets for lying outside at night and camping. We would head for the front yard, where there were few trees to block the sky. In the back yard, you had to contend with the smells of the old toilet and the hog lot. Those things had only one value about them and that is the smelly truth.

We drank up a lot of Kool-Aid. Daddy drank other things. Kool-Aid was not real healthy for him, he said, but was just right for kids. We would just lie on our backs looking up and seeing who could find the most satellites. We saw shooting stars and all of the craters on the moon and learned the names of the stars and planets. Sometimes Elmer would have to wake me up to go in the house and go to bed. Once in a while I would wake up in the morning with a thick pile of old blankets weighting me down and dewdrops on the ends of my stubble of hair. Again, every old dog for a mile would be sleeping on the blankets with me. They sure smelled bad, but I think I would have missed them if they had not found me in the night. I always wondered where they slept when I wasn't out with quilts. Mom would hang the old quilts on the outside clothesline to get the dog smell out. Never know — we might need them again tonight.

Old Jim the Dog

One Saturday morning, my coon-hunting partners took me with them to visit friends of theirs that lived in some unknown, lost kind of place. It was so far out in the country that you would have to go to town just to fish. All I could think of was that I sure hoped they knew the way home. We had gone to look at a litter of black and tan coon dog puppies that had been born a day or two earlier. We walked over to the doghouse, and the man hollered for his daughter. A little girl about my age climbed out of the doghouse. They laughed at her in a kind of nice way. I thought, "If all of you men were not here, I would like to climb in there with her and play with them puppies, too."

There were nine little puppy dogs just hollering their heads off. They were about the size of a large mouse or possibly a small rat, but no bigger. Their eyes were not even open yet. Every one of them looked like its head had been born first, and the rest grew in behind it. The mother dog was young, too, and had only five tits working, so three puppies had to go. I said that I would take one. I was told that they would take lots of care, since they could not even see where they were.

I named my pup "Jim" as soon as I picked him up. His pappy's name was Big Jim Dog, and he was a solid eighty pounder. Young Jim was no bigger than a very large mouse, and I put him in my shirt pocket. He screamed like a wild cat all the way home. The fleas jumped off of him onto me, but I did not care. He was my coon dog pup, and I liked him and I had had fleas before and Momma had lots of lye soap. He grew to be named "Old Jim."

When I took him home, Mom put him in a fishbowl for the night. That little dog howled like a real coon dog or something. No one slept, not one wink. The next day we started him out on baby milk. Mom and everyone fed him about every hour. We even got up in the night to feed him. By the end of the week, everyone said that he had to go outside to the doghouse. Between the howling and the fleas, he was getting the best of us. Mom put him out in the dog pen with a flea collar around his stomach. In less than a year he was big. When he was fully grown, just like his daddy, he weighed more than 80 pounds.

In every way Jim looked the part of a coon dog. But he wasn't much of a coon dog at all. Old Jim's hunting skills were a lot like Old Mouse's — pretty near worthless. He was my dog for truck riding and my mother's lap dog. Yeah, Jim took hunting lessons from Mouse for sure. I'm sure he was afraid of the dark, too, because like me he liked to stay in the house or barn at night. This is real bad trait for a coon dog

Jim was a member of the family. He went freely into and out of the house. One of the funniest things was that when it thundered, someone had to run fast to open a door. Mom learned the hard way about Jim's fear of thunder. A sudden storm came up, and Jim ran right through the screen door and into Mom and Daddy's bedroom. He climbed under her bed and would not come out. Mom had to drag the trembling rascal out.

At the old cabin on the river, the only heat I had was a fireplace. On cold nights, I would make a very large fire, which might warm about half of the cabin to the point you couldn't see your breath. You had to find Jim before you went to bed. If you didn't find him, you were going to wake up cold. Old Jim dog would put his head against the door and push it open. Then he would go to the brick hearth and go to sleep in front of the fire while the snow blew in the door. He could not be taught to close the door.

One time, Old Jim got locked in the cabin and stayed there for two whole days. No one missed him. He was prone to running off in search of female dogs wanting to go courting. When I opened the door, the romantic rascal ran straight for the river. He would drink water for a while, pee for a while and crap for a while. After a few minutes he was all filled up again and all emptied out again. But, he never took a dump in the house. My bed was full of dog hair, fleas and dog dirt. I had to wash everything and set the mattress out in the sun to freshen up.

Jim always obliged courting females. Billy Holston had a female in heat one time, so he locked her up in one of the many old junk cars on his farm. He went to feed her one morning, and found out Jim had gotten into the car. Mr. Holston said that he had eaten his way in through a door. When the pups were born they were "black enough to pee ink," he said.

Mom and Old Jim did a lot of things together — like building a fire in the barbeque grill to fix a picnic for my Aunt Doris. Now stop right here. Don't you think Mom could have found a better helper for a cookout? Well, where she went he went. When the fire was just right, Mom took to deboning and trimming the fat from eight or ten steaks. Old Jim Dog obliged Mom by eating all of the fat and bones. She then carefully laid them steaks on the grill. Truly they covered the entire top of the grill.

Mom left Jim in charge while she went back in the cabin for salt and pepper. When she came back, Jim had knocked the grill over and had eaten each and every one of them hot steaks. He was just lying on his side near to the grill with a big bulge in his stomach. Mom took to cussing, and Jim took to running. Mom was chasing him, chopping at him with a yard rake. Jim would run a few feet and set down. When Mom got close, he would get up and run a few more feet. I think Mom could have caught him if she had run a little harder and cussed a little less.

When Old Jim was around you never had to worry about finding someone to go for a canoe ride with you. He would just jump in and sit in the front like he was the ship's captain. Heck, he was captain. He rode and I did all the work. When he got hot, he would just jump out without any warning at all. One time he turned over the canoe jumping out. He also would run down the river, chasing deer and rabbits along the way. One whistle, and he would be standing on the bank waiting for you to come pick him up. He was generally covered in mud and stinking to the high heavens.

Old Jim thought that it was great when he happened upon a dead deer or dead groundhog. He just loved to roll on their remains. He thought it smelled like Chanel No. 5 or something. I took to only carrying tomatoes and baked sweet potatoes for food on these little trips. The only thing that he would not eat was tomatoes and sweet potatoes.

Now, Old Jim loved to ride. One time a young lady had come to the house. Later that night, when she drove home, a few miles from the house she felt a cold and dark presence in the car with her. Before she could scream or stop or jump out, the presence touched her on the back of the neck with a cold wet nose and barked real loud. The next day, when this lady brought Old Jim back home, he was setting up front like he owned the world. Well, he did, I reckon. He had his head stuck out the window with his big ears waving in the wind. He also had his belly full of good table scraps. As the story was relayed to me: "When he touched my neck and barked, I thought that I was going to soak my panties." Well, he did have that effect on some people.

When Old Jim came of age, he was on the bottom of the pecking order. Chuck had two hounds, Rowdy and Jake. Old Rowdy was the top dog, and he knew it. Jake was clearly number two. Every morning it seemed like these three hounds had to sniff each other and growl at each other. Often they would nip at each other. If one of the dogs did not agree with the current arrangement, watch out, there was going to be a dogfight. Each and every time, Old Rowdy got things back in order real quick. One morning after one of these dog pecking order sessions, Jake came out the top dog and Rowdy and Jim had to now take orders. A year or so later, there was another one of those real loud fights to see who was going to be the top dog. This time Old Jim was the winner, and Old Rowdy and now Jake were on the bottom.

I tell you this because I learned from them old dogs. Dogs are truly not as dumb as we sometimes make them out to be. They have a way of getting right to the heart of the matter bothering them and a clear way of straightening things out. I sometimes wish people were a little more direct, kind of like old Rowdy was. Not so much fighting it out; but just said what was on their mind and let the pieces fall where they needed to.

A Coon Dog Show
and a Real Night Hunt!

I am guessing that I was all of ten years old when I went to my first night hunt. These events are real big and very important in the Coon Hunting World. You see, by now I was receiving a monthly coon-hunting magazine. The title was *Full Cry*, or something like that. I read it from cover to cover, and every day I looked at the advertisements for stud dogs, puppies for sale, and events around the region. I dreamed of seeing a dog in *Full Cry* that I knew. I also knew that I would never in my life be so lucky as to own one. Combine this magazine and the county store and you get yourself a real education in the world of coon hunting.

Like with humans, you got to learn where you are born, your starting place, and what your lot in life is thought to be. Some are going to make it and some just ain't. The real hard part for a ten-year-old is defining the word "it." "It" seems to move a lot in meaning, if you know what I'm talking about. You see, "it" was no different for a coon dog. He either had it or he did not have it. If he did not have it, he was just about worthless. But Old Thunder had "it" and he knew it. I just loved to look at him and marvel.

Now, a night hunt is an organized activity for real, or as we call them in the profession "diehard," coon hunters. I had been hunting for a long time myself, probably upwards of two or three years, but real hard for only one year. I knew what was going on, but that was about all I knew. This was a real learning experience. I was well up on my dog talking lingo too: a dog (a male dog), a bitch (a female dog), first strike (the first dog to start to barking on a coon track), running trash (chasing animals other than a coon), a hot track versus a cold track, and treed (when the dogs run a coon up a tree). Most important of all was the beautiful sound of your dog barking as hard as it could while tracking a coon. The change in its voice told the hunter what was going on from a mile or more away and whose dog was a-doing it.

Another thing, I never heard of a raccoon until I went to school in Blacksburg. Out in the county where I lived, they were just coons. Down at Tom Long's Store, all the coons were long-legged, fast runners, good climbers, capable of swimming a mile and more than willing to jump from one tree to the next. Another thing about our coons, they were not scared of any of our blue ticks, red bones or black and tans. About the only thing tougher was the 20-gauge shotgun that set in the corner behind the broom.

A real coon dog is a breed of its own. I am not meaning one specific breed of dog here. I mean any breed of hound that was trained to run all night long from dusk to sun-up — any blue tick that can take a two-day-old track and work it for hours until he is licking at the new made footprints of a coon. Every once in a while, hunters will come across a very long-eared black and tan with a sense of smell so keen that he could pick up even the slightest trace of coon scent on a creek or an almost dry branch. He could work the stream and bank until he would be standing in the exact spot where a boar coon got himself a drink of water at daylight the day before. That rascal would correctly follow the cold track until he was running in a high lop on a hot trail. A 70-pound red bone that settles back on his or her haunches and barks real steady under the tree until we would get there would have the sense to know if the coon had jumped out of the tree to another and was off and running again. These were the dogs I am speaking of when I say "the breed of coon dogs." They stood all alone at the top of the pecking order. Not every dog that wore the collar or had the papers earned this title. No sir.

Even today, 50 years later, if I were to stand at the gas station in Long Shop and say the names Thunder, Joe, Ranger, Queeny, Old Muse and Rawhide, there would be a short silence in the store. Then the group would erupt into many stories of these dogs' exploits. Every red-necked boy and man knew these dogs and others just like them.

In the early afternoon, just after dinner had been eaten (back then dinner, not lunch, was eat at 12:00), it was time for the water race. You would hear men and women say things like

"I can bet you my firstborn pup from the next litter that Old Jack is faster that than your Racer!"

"Not true neither. Here, put a $10.00 bill right there and set a rock on them. Whoever's dog is the fastest can move the rock off-en of that money."

All around the pond there would be bets of all kinds. Just as soon as the tension was as high as it could get, the crowd would get quiet and someone would show up with a coon in a wire cage. Two men would put a boat in the water. One person would paddle the boat across the pond, while the other man let the coon's feet touch the water. On the other side, the coon cage was then pulled up into a big tree deep in the woods.

Everyone turned their dog loose at the same time. The objective is, first off, find where the coon entered the water, then swim across the pond following the coon scent. Second: find the tree where the coon is setting. Points were awarded first, second, third and so on. While they were always important, points did not matter as much as who beat whom. And who got to lift that rock holding down the $20.00. Grown men would argue, and I would just set back and take it all in.

I have seen grown men take their dogs jogging every night, just to build up their lungs and improve their endurance for this event. I even saw an older man tie his dog to his car's bumper and drive down the road real slow for a mile or two. He was toughening up his dog. I tell you this to let you know this was serious fun. Fine dogs, with strong hearts and willing bodies, were just sold to the highest bidder because they swam slow. They were deemed to be "no count and just simply did not have it." They showed that they were not of the coon-hunting breed, so they got culled! Winners were chosen as potential mates.

Late in the afternoon there was a dog show. Now, I am right sure that you have watched the dog show on television or maybe at the fair. You know, the shows where men and ladies almost look like their dogs. Both have little bows and combs in their hair. They run in a little circle and jump over a little hurdle. Well, a coon dog show is nothing like this.

Dogs were washed and shampooed and combed up real slick so they'd just shine in the sunlight. Loose and shaggy hairs were carefully cut off. I was told not to get near the dogs when they are on the stand. They don't put up with much crap. (Other expletives were used here, but I don't want to hurt your eyes or ears.) Them SOBs will kill you or me or anything else when they want to. So I just stayed up on the bank away from them.

Then the dogs were stood on small tables about four feet off of the ground. They were just slumped over humps of hounds until the owners came over and touched them. On command they stood up equally on all four feet and raised their lion-eyed heads as if to announce to the other dogs "I am the He Bull in These Here Woods." One after the other, each dog showed his or her prowess, flexing their muscles for all to see, just like they were a canine Charles Atlas. They were judged on their form and on how well they had been trained. People took note

118

of a winner and thought real careful-like about this animal as a mate for their prize-winning dog or bitch. "These pups could make me some money, but just wait until after the night hunt before I make any decisions," owners would mumble.

Sometime later each hunter drew a number from a can. Hunters were divided into groups of four by their random numbers. Buddies and neighbors could not hunt in the same group. Each group had a group leader, who had the final say on the hunt. Their rules held fast. Each number had a set area of the county to hunt. At a set time everybody started, and everyone was required to be back at the hunt club office at 12:30 or 1:00 a.m. for the awarding of the trophies.

Because I was just ten years old, no one seemed to mind if I went, too. I was with a local hunter who had borrowed a dog from a friend. From now on until the trophy was awarded, there was no laughter, idle talk or lollygagging; this was real serious stuff. Now, I am going to change the names here so no one gets the wrong idea. It was rumored that two grown men and maybe even some boys may have been shot for misquoting a dog's name or action. So, me and Huckleberry loaded up in the truck with "Old Clyde." At about 7:00 p.m. we arrived at Holler Number 6, and everyone held their dogs on leashes. Them dogs just kind of laid around and sniffed the air like they were getting their bearings. The leaders said: "Boys, you can turn them loose." In far less than a heartbeat, them sleepy dogs came to life like they were running for their lives. They knew the score; this wasn't their first rodeo, and they were ready for a run.

The dogs take out at a pretty fast pace, so we as a group take out at a pretty fast pace, too. I'm breathing real hard. The men just smoke one cigarette after another and keep on running. They are just about as fast as their dogs. I am happy to run in back of the pack of men, except for the limbs and twigs that keep on hitting me in the face and ears.

All of a sudden, there is one solitary bark, then another. I look right in the eyes of Huckleberry. I know that bark is Old Clyde. He has struck something. By the rule as I heard, someone has got to say: "Strike my dog." I am just waiting for the call. Old Clyde is pretty much a straight dog, but I must admit there was something strange in the bark. I look right into the eyes of Huckleberry, and he looks away. I know that he knows that it is Old Clyde. Here are some real powerful, hard-to-match points — first strike and all. In the next second or two, Old Clyde is going to bark, and someone has got to claim the dog. I wait for the bark and call, but neither one comes. Then it dawns on me that Old Clyde was running trash for a step or two. She has jumped a rabbit off of the nest or crossed a possum. If we had called "Strike," Old Clyde would now be on the dog leash and headed for the truck.

In just a few minutes, we cross a small body of water — you know, larger than a branch, but much smaller than a creek. All of a sudden, the mountain comes alive with dog-barking. "Strike" the first one, "Strike" the second one, "Strike" the third dog. Every dog is on the same track and running like the mountain is on fire, but not one sound from Old Clyde. In a few seconds, he chimes in. But, he is at least a half a mile below the pack.

Old Clyde puts the hammer down, and within five or six minutes he has caught up with the pack. People say: "Whose dog is that? That SOB is fast." Then, like a fool, I chime in: "That is Old Clyde, and he is real fast." About the time I speak, Old Clyde takes the lead and starts to move ahead of the pack. On the record, he strikes forth, but is first to the tree by a quarter of mile. All that jogging everyday behind a car pays off. When we get to the tree, I just kind of want to go pet him and hug him around the neck, but Huckleberry tells me to stand clear: "Them other dogs are real pissed off that he came from out of nowhere and beat them to the tree."

I did get to put the leash on him and lead him from the tree. Hell, I felt at least six or maybe seven feet tall. Holy macaroni! This is what a real coon dog does, and I have now seen it and done it. I now realize that I have some of "it," too.

For the rest of the night, the men ran like men possessed. They tried to stay up with the dogs. The more coons we crossed, the greater the chance they will earn points. Old Clyde did lose a "first to the strike," but none could beat him to the tree. Out in the distance, an awful commotion broke out. I did not know what was happening, but all of the men did. This bunch of cigarette-smoking, chubby men just broke into a hard run to their dogs. One of the dogs had literally run down the coon, and the others had joined in the fight. The old coon was up on a small tree or bush. When dogs would jump up, the coon would scratch their noses and ears. All four were somewhat scratched up when we got there. Dogs are strong and have many teeth. But coons are agile and can hold on with one paw and scratch with three, while they also bite.

On the ground, I did not know if this old coon could whip four dogs, but it had the high ground and was taking full advantage of it. When I put the leash on Old Clyde, I was kind of scared that big-eyed toothy rascal would bite me, so I was fast with my snap! At 1:00 a.m. Huckleberry was awarded the trophy for our group. But I was truly amazed that we, or should I say Old Clyde, did not earn the winning trophy. I was left wondering what went on during that hunt! Yes, I would be back.

Just because a dog lost at swimming and lost on the show stand or made poor showing in the hunting phase did not mean that there wasn't still some market value. The hunts were also attended by men who bought good-looking dogs. There were the dealers in secondhand dog flesh who would change the name, fatten them up some or thin them down some. Change them a little was all that was needed. The most remarkable part of this process was the marketing.

A few visits to the numerous country stores, asking who was paying the best price for coon hides, and a great story about last week's hunt set the stage for building up a dog's credentials. "Why, Old Wild Bill took that cold track and would not quit. Two times I started to pull him off. I was starting to get cold and a little hungry, had to get up early, too. Just about the time I was about to put the chain on him, he would pick up the pace. Worked that track for two hours or so, he did." Before you knew it, this salesman was easing back toward the scales and out the door. He never once said that Old Wild Bill caught or treed that coon; but about everybody knew he had. You could almost see the hunt as he talked.

Before anyone could even ask one question, the seller would just get up and leave the store and wait for someone with a real poor or trash running dog to show up at his house wanting to buy Bill. Some small-time coon hunters just wanted to trade up for a better dog, kind of like trading up for a better used car. Coon dog sellers were skilled talkers and even more skilled traders. The process was fun to watch and hear. Almost everyone, even the purchaser, knew that they were being taken advantage of, but went on and bought the reject coon dogs.

Yes, I even got caught one time too. This little blue tick bitch's given name was "Jenny." I just called her Jenny, too, so as not to confuse her any more. Her number-one selling trait was, "She can roll over. Any dog that can roll over on command is sharper than a rat turd." So said the owner.

Never once did I see any hunting traits demonstrated. I paid twenty hard-earned dollars for this mangy little blue tick. Only one time did I ever see her tree anything. She caught an opossum; no coon.

Soon she started getting as big and round as a bucket. After about a month, she had a litter of nine puppies. I had to almost pay people to take them! She would not hunt, and I did not know who the pappy of them pups was. No one wanted them. Elmer said, "It serves you right. You ort to not be so trusting. Mr. So and So, he knew she was going to have them puppies, and he unloaded her on the first fool that came along and that was you. You got to learn that people will crap (he did not say a kind word like crap) on you. Even your friends will crap on you when money is involved." I have found this to not always be true. But there is some truth in Elmer's warning. There is good reason to be on your toes when a coon dog is involved.

P.S. There was one puppy we named "Ugly." His head was kind of on crooked-like, and he was knock-kneed a might. But, he sure could eat. Ugly just loved everybody that came to the house. He grew to be real good dog, for what, I do not have a clue. I pawned him off on a man from Floyd County with just one good story. Pick of the litter he was, and the last one of them pups. As soon as they were weaned, people just showed up to take them others. I wanted to keep Ugly for myself, but now Elmer said he had to go. Then I just set back and got even dumber than I was. This man left thinking that he had just taken advantage of a dumb, fat boy, not so little of a kid. I told the story at Tom Long's store like the grown men, and they all laughed.

The Lovely Miss Gail asked "Why did your parents let you go to this event?" Well, Mom and Daddy had very few criteria for my activities. First of all, by age ten I had done been turned out and was kind of on my own. I kind of came and went as I wanted. Second, they did not care much where I went as long as I would be gone for long periods of time. If I was out running the mountain all Friday night, I'd sleep most of Saturday getting ready for Saturday night. Then, I'd sleep most of Sunday. Mom and Dad had that weekend knocked out. Then came grade school on Monday morning.

Miss Gail asked, "Where in the world did you learn about this stuff?" By night, there were a lot to be learned at the old country stores.

Thinking about this, I was left wondering what in the world a town boy would do on Friday and Saturday nights? I just never asked one. I guess they, too, went coon hunting.

Another thing here: Old Jim sure did look the part of a coon dog. He had them long black and tan features. You know, the beautiful long ears and strong body. It was a true pleasure to watch him run. He was sleek and graceful and was a pretty good dog-fighter, too. Jim had a deep chest with a wide spread. He had pure breed papers to prove his lineage. But the truth was, his actions proved he was not and was never going to be one of the "Coon Dog Breed." He was nothing more than a house dog. He just did not have "it." A good dealer in dog flesh just might have talked him into a good kennel, but me and Mama Ruth just liked him the way he was.

The Hair Cut!

When I was in the fourth grade, I decided that I was going to grow a new hairstyle — a set of "ducktails" like the big boys on the school bus. When I set about hair growing, I found it to be slow going. Every day my hair was just about the same; no new growth, and what little hair I had stuck straight up like wire.

I decided to take matters into my own hands. If I wanted the "ducktail" look, I would have to grease it down; so I went to Mason Williams' barbershop and got two cans of this stuff called "Butch Hair Cream." It was a little thicker than petroleum jelly and smelled very much like strong strawberry jelly. The gnats and bees were always getting stuck on my head. Now, keep in mind that my hair was no more than one inch long. Good "ducktails" required at least five or six inches of hair. To make up the difference, I used a lot of Butch Hair Cream. My hair was thick and shiny with grease and smelled like someone was canning strawberry jelly. "Good God Almighty, what have you gone and done to your head?" bellowed Elmer. "Something has just got to be done about this!"

Elmer and Colman Hilton caught me up and scrubbed my head two times with strong soap, just to get the Butch Hair Cream out. Before I could even run, Elmer took out a pair of hair clippers and cut my hair down to a length of about 1/50 of an inch. If you were to train your eye up real close on my head, you might pick up a little fuzz. When I ran my hand over my head it felt like the stiff wire brushes used to clear a double bastard file. When I looked in the mirror, I saw my head was as white as snow. I was a sight. Elmer and Colman hollered and laughed, "Look at that white head with that big nose!" Me, I just took off for the river. I thought I just would never go back, but about dark I did. I had no hair and no duck tails either. I did have something else though: an awfully sunburnt head.

The next morning the sunburn blisters were taller than my hair. Come Monday morning, I did not have to go to school. Momma kept me home, because the blisters on my head were even worse. They were touching each other and leaking out water. Mamaw and Momma greased my head with one of Mamaw's herbal poultices. I think they packed my head in jule weed poultice. I was a sight! Also, Momma sent a note to school explaining my sunburnt head to the teachers. I did not know that the teacher read the note to my class and asked my classmates not to laugh when I came in with a no-hair, a sun-blistered head and the whole thing covered with a jule weed poultice. Which was held on with a skullcap.

My close friend, Terry Albert, walked up to the teacher's desk and told her to just go ahead and set his butt on fire with that big paddle of hers, because he was going to laugh at me and that was all there was to it. The next morning when I walked in, the whole class busted out laughing at me. There was no holding back at all; they just roared. The teacher laughed a lot, too. Well, I kind of laughed a little with them. But rest assured there was no sympathy for a little boy with no ducktails and a sunburnt head. Especially one with a smelly bunch of weeds stuck on his head.

Momma said to Elmer, "Aren't you ashamed of yourself for embarrassing that boy that way, and that he has a badly sunburnt head to boot?"

Elmer replied, "Got them ducktails off-en his head, didn't I? There ain't no long-haired hippies going to live around here!"

In less than a month, the blisters were gone and the laughter had stopped. The fuzz on my head had started to take root again, and I haired over nicely. But every once in awhile someone would look my way and start one of those great big, gut-busting laughs. There was no need to ask what was so funny.

I just never did get back around to trying to grow them ducktails. By the time I was big enough and old enough and had about enough hair, they had gone out of style. So, I just stuck with my skin-close crew cut. No, there never was no long-haired hippie at our house.

Maple Syrup, I Think

When I was growing up, my parents thought that anything that did not kill you only made you stronger. I guess this story will fit well right here. We ate a lot of pancakes, and I did like them. But we ate them not because we liked them, but because hey were quick to make and cheap. There were seven mouths to feed in that small, four-room cinderblock house, and cost was always a top priority. I loved maple syrup, too.

Each month, Mom received two books in the mail for us children. Somehow she just knew that would make us better people. One was a history book, and the other was a science book. One of the history books had a section on New England and making maple syrup. All of the men on the hill said that there were plenty of maples around here to make syrup, but it took a lot of sap. To make one gallon of syrup, it took about 75 gallons of maple sap and a week to boil it down.

Well, I was not up too much on my tree identification. One day in February, I was down near the railroad gate climbing trees. I broke a limb out of a tree that I thought was a maple.

The sap just poured out of it. I ran up to the trash pile by the old junk car and got a right clean can or two. I wiped them clean with leaves, set one at the end of the broken limb and left it to fill. The drops were coming fast. In less than an hour, my old peach can was about full, and I set the other one under the drip. In a little while the other one was nearly half full. I was in the maple syrup business for sure.

The flaw in my business plan was that my maple tree was a balsawood tree. Locals just called them "lynn trees." I did not know this. Well, someone needed to test the strength of my maple sap. Since I was the only employee, I guessed I was the taste-tester, too. I picked up the first can to drink the sap, and I drank it all. It was about the nastiest stuff I ever tasted. In just a minute or two, I was sicker than a dog trying to pass a peach seed. I had a real serious case of diarrhea and vomiting. Stuff shot from both ends of me with great force. I was laid up sick for a day or two. The more I explained my sickness, the more Elmer just shook his head. Uncle Shorty and Nelson just rolled and laughed. Mom said, "One of these days, you are going to do something that is going to kill you or give you rabies or something even worse."

Another of life's lessons: only try to make maple syrup from sugar maple trees Also, rinse the peach cans from the dump in the river. Another suggestion: boil the sap before you drink it. Better yet, go over to the Piggly Wiggly Grocery Store and just buy a jar of maple syrup once in a while. Take it from me; it will be a lot better.

I Once Did Like to Play with Bees

Yes, for some reason I did like to play with bees. I was not too much interested in honeybees, like normal children. I liked them baldfaced hornets, yellow jackets, and large and small bumblebees. Occasionally, I even was known to play with a nest of little bumblebees. Bees just caught my attention and would not turn it a-loose until they stung me.

My first remembering of bees was of a large paper hornets' nest under the eaves of the old barn. Every time I fed the hogs with Shorty, we would look at the nest. It seemed to be getting bigger. "Damn you boy, stay the hell away from them hellions while I am around you," Shorty would say.

I reckon he could read my mind. "If they are that bad, why don't you knock down the nest and kill them?" I asked.

"Boy, you just can't, because them are mean little sons of bitches. God only knows why, but He put them here for some reason," Shorty would explain. "You leave them alone, and they will leave you alone. Come winter, they will be gone. Besides they ain't bothering you none."

One of my many little jobs, created for me to do, was to hoe the tomato patch near the barn and bust up all the clay clods with a little two-pound ball peen hammer. I know I was no more than eight or nine years old, and Miss Guinn, my fourth grade teacher, was always informing me: "You know you are far too big for your age, and I think that makes you too curious for your own good. You just wait. One of these days your curiosity is going to jump up and bite you."

The more I chopped weeds and hammered them clods, the more them baldfaced hornets took to worrying me. You know the ones I am talking about: the black ones with white rings around their butts, and the white face and kind of wide eyes. Well, I found myself looking down into the metal rain barrel watching them wiggle-tails, with them bees overhead. I just watched the bees go in and out. I was wondering what was going on in the paper nest. Miss Guinn was getting more right all the time. There I was barefooted, with no shirt on, just the little homemade, feed-sack shorts.

My plan was to tear a small hole in the nest, one just big enough to stick my eyes to, so I could see what was going on. Heck, them bees would never know. I started looking for a tool. I decided to break off a limb from a wild cherry tree right beside the old rain barrel. I reached up and grabbed the wild cherry limb and swung down on it so that I could break it. Well, the limb did not break, but it did manage to hit the nest and tear it clean into. There must have been a few less than three million bees in the nest. They were on me like white on rice, and run I did. I was moving as fast as fat little legs would take me, and every once in a while one would sting me. One even got me on the ear. A time or two, they got me on my back. I learned that back stings are the worst. There ain't time to stop and roll on the ground or scrub your back on a tree to knock them off. Remember, I did not have a shirt on. You got to take the pain and hope you outlive them hornets. I ran right to Mamaw's house; it was the closest one. Grandmother took a dishtowel and knocked them hornets off and painted me with wet baking soda and a jule weed poultice. She did not approve of chewing tobacco, even for bee stings.

The funny thing was that she was not too much worried about me. She was more concerned about the wild cherry limb and where was it right then. She did not want the horse, cow or hogs eating the wilted leaves, because those leaves could make livestock sick. I was sent back a little later with a small hand saw to cut the limb and drag it to the house for Grandmother to inspect. The bees were still pissed off, you might say. Shorty and Elmer went down there that night and burned them out. Bee stings just did not bother me much back then. But it made me feel bad when Daddy and Shorty took turns hollering at me.

"I told you to bust up them clods, didn't I?"

Then the other one would start hollering, "If I told you once, I must have told you ten times, them are mean little sons-of-bitches. I guess you now know that don't you?"

You can always tell who your family is; they are the ones that get to holler at you when you mess up. Uncle Shorty must have been real close kin!

The Last of the True Blackberry Pickers

Where we lived, there were lots of blackberries, and one summer I got it into my head to make some sort of industry out of picking them. No one but me was dumb enough to get themselves into this!! I would get started and pick steadily until it got really hot. . .or until I got to thinking about being snake bit. . .or getting stung really badly by yellow jackets or hornets. . .or possibly being dragged off by Big Foot.

The damnedest critter in the world is a chigger. It is a little red bug about the size if a needle's point. It can dig deeply into your skin and leave a welt about the size of a buck marble. It will stay sore about a week and itches like hell. I will not tell you all of the places that I had chigger bites. But the ones farther south do itch and have a tendency to get really sore and you cannot see them to scratch very well. At one time, I had more than 15 big chigger bites on me. The only known treatment for a chigger bite is sitting in the river and lots of lye soap. I think that you just have got to drown them rascals.

If I was a long time in the berry patches, no one would

come looking for me unless they thought my buckets were full. Grownups weren't going to take the chance of getting eaten by chiggers and stung by bees, or chased by black snakes. The fact was, I was on my own picking them blackberries. I bet Old Big Footed Sasquatch could have come by, and wouldn't have come into that patch either.

Butwhat bothered me the most were the gnats and the mosquitoes. They would get into your eyes and come close to blinding you. Between sweat and the gnats, I don't know which was worse. The killer was when one of them would fly down your ear and buzz around. He would get stuck in your earwax or just fly around in the dark void. They are very hard to dig out.

That was why Shorty would slap his ear. I had a treatment for the gnats and mosquitoes. I smoked lots of cigarettes and cheap cigars, so that the smoke would keep them off'n of me. Now the meanest insect I ever did battle with is a horse fly. I had one of them massive bloodsuckers light on my back. I did not feel the thing until he was about finished. I had to take a stick and rub my back to knock him off.

Now, please don't get me started on ticks! Each day after I had sold the blackberries, I would have to go to the river and wash off the insects and fish a little just to build up my energy for tomorrow's blackberries.

Every day on my way to the patch, I would stop by Mason Williams' barbershop and buy me 10 or 12 five-cent,

King Edward or Swisher Sweets Cigars and a pack of filtered Winstons. I liked them better than unfiltered Lucky Strikes or Camels, but in a pinch I would smoke those, too. I had to get a plug of Bull of the Woods and a can of Prince Albert and papers at one of the stores in Long Shop. There was no question about it: you had to have these things or the bugs would eat you. I asked Daddy to get them for me. If I showed up, I would get another blackberry order. No other idiot would do this for 50 cents a gallon.

You tried to be at the berry patch before the dew lifted. I wanted to be out of the patch by 1:00 p.m., because then it was getting hot. Daddy said "You don't want the berries to get too hot." He was a lot more worried about the berries than he was about me. Hell, I was worried more about me.

After I'd walked a mile or possibly two miles or more back home or to someone's house with ten gallons of berries, the old women would say: "You know, you have mashed them berries. The ones on the bottom are all mashed, and they are ruined." Or maybe: "Well, I'll pick the good ones off of the top and buy them from you. The rest just pour over into these kettles. They are no good, and I'm not going to buy them."

I learned to just tell them to leave the berries they didn't want in the bucket. Sometimes I would set down in their yard and drink the warm berry juice. Sometimes I would take it home for Tootie or Grandmother or Mom to make jelly out of. The truth of the matter is I learned that some old ladies would lie to me and cheat me out of my blackberry juice.

Another thing: berry picking isn't profitable at all. I lost money; I spent more money on Bull of the Woods, cigarettes, cigars and pipe tobacco than I took in. I still did not have two nickels in my pockets. But I was fatter. I had eaten so many blackberry pies and desserts that it was a profitable picking season in another way.

The only human being on this earth that had a worse summer job than me picking blackberries was poor old Jerry Noonkester. Jerry had a job cutting and stacking firewood for Miss Lottie Wilkens. She lived right at the start of the Keester Branch Road. After he had cut and stacked wood for a couple of days, Miss Lottie came and paid him off with a dime. She said "I think that will buy you a bottle of pop."

You Want to Go Swimming

When I was a child, my brothers and sisters and I went to the swimming hole on Lena Long's farm in Tom's Creek about every Saturday and Sunday. Elmer did like to play with us kids. He was real good at it, too. He tried, and I give him credit for that. First, he would slip out to the toilet and to the old "building" to pick up whatever liquor he had, which he would hide up under the front driver's seat of the Carryall. I guess he did not want anyone to know that he was drinking, driving and swimming. Then he would let out a war whoop call to see if anyone wanted to go swimming. Once we were all loaded up, he stopped at each house where there were kids and asked if they wanted to join us. Their parents were also invited. Sometimes there would be 15 or 16 people in the Carryall, excuse me, in the Suburban.

When we got to the creek over by Lena Long's, swimming lessons started. By 4 or 5 years of age I was an okay swimmer, and I did not have to participate in these games anymore. Most of them were real playful. I have seen Daddy swim for an hour with one of my brothers or sisters lying on his back. He would dive deep, and they would float off. After a while, they would take a stroke or two. I also saw kids get into the deeper part of the swimming hole and be struggling. The adults would have to take a sip and watch for second or two before they came to the rescue. "You keep swimming, and you will make it. I'll be along in a minute."

I was always happy when Daddy got hungry. The whole wet crowd would pile back into the van to drive deep into the woods near Poverty Creek to an old store. Elmer would go in and return with a Royal Crown Cola or Double Cola for everyone. He also had a box and everyone knew what was in it — Kern's oatmeal cakes and big wheel of Longhorn cheese. We would pull up on the side of the road under a big white pine tree, where each person got a cake and big hunk of cheese and a cold drink. Then we would wade in the spring branch near Chock and Annie Bell's house and look for fossil rocks.

Life was good! I truly thought that everyone did this stuff. Now I think this, too, was one of the true Lytton traditions. I personally keep this tradition going; I still eat oatmeal and cheese cakes. Today, the Old Ira Morris Store building is still standing, though it has been empty for many years. I see the boards over the windows, but I still remember what it once was. It brought me a lot of joy!

When I hear the story about two brothers (not mine) who were swimming at the Big Hole, I think back to my family swimming at Lena Long's Creek. The Big Hole is in Long Shop just behind the Lutheran Church. I was well on the way to being almost grown. I do not know the exact date; but if I was at the Big Hole I had done been turned out. You see, when I was little, the Big Hole was one of the places I was not permitted to go.

Everyone was up on the bank practicing their smoking skills, me included. The older of the two brothers, Rooster, was setting on the creek bank smoking a cigarette. Tootsy, the younger, was swimming. He was a very poor swimmer. When Rooster looked up and saw that his younger brother was drowning he barked: "Help Tootsy, jump in and help Tootsy. He is drowning. I got another drag on this cigarette, and I cannot go until I finish this cigarette." That was kind of like Daddy leaving you to fend for yourself while he got himself another nip. Life has its priorities.

I did wade out with the others to pull Old Tootsy in. He was no worse off for the experience. Rooster died when he was about 25 years old. From what I have been told, he was drunk and fell asleep in the back of pickup truck one winter night and froze to death. Old Tootsy just kind of faded into the past. I never even knew his real name.

Be Damn Careful Who You Go Siccing Your Dog On

I am about 10 years old and wanting in the worst kind of way to become a tried and true professional coon hunter. For the past nights I have had my little blue tick hound named Jenny down on the Tommy Bottom coon hunting. Now, Jenny is just a little better coon dog than Old Jim. Once in while she will tree an opossum, and even more rarely she will tree a real coon. But she was a really good barker. You could hear her for a long way.

On this very night I have walked back up the Tommy Bottom, and Jenny has treed a possum near Leroy Lucas' spring, but it wasn't worth shooting out of the tree. That was about it for the night. The 12:30 shift whistle has blown at the Radford Arsenal, so it was time to head for home. Car traffic would soon be becoming down the road. I walked on up the Tommy Road and turned down the hard top. I was just passing the Ted Reed house, when Ted opened the door a little and sicked his old big dog on me. Before I could even think about running, the big dog bit me on the leg, just above the knee. I just happened to be finishing off my last Double Cola. I hit the big dog on the head three or four times with the pop bottle as hard as I could.

Each time I hit the dog's head, it sounded like a cantaloupe being dropped onto the floor; kind of like a dull thud. He was still biting, and I was still hitting as hard as I could. After a few licks on the head, the Old Big Dog turned me loose and walked off slowly. I sure did not like being dog bit, and I don't think this dog liked being worked over on the head with pop bottle! Another funny this is, I dropped Daddy's 12-gauge on the road. I guess I could have shot that mean dog if I had thought of it. I might have shot my own leg off, too.

I grabbed up Daddy's gun, little Jenny and ran home. I got both Mom and Daddy up to tell them what had just happened. Mom and Daddy washed my dog bite with lots of soap and water a few times. They exchanged a few sharp looks between them. Mom rubbed a thick layer of Raleigh Salve on my leg and tied it up with old sheet rags and sent me to bed. All I could think was thank goodness they did not call Grandmother; she might have wanted to amputate or worse. You just never knew about her or what some of her treatments were going to be. Some were on the drastic side.

While I was doing all the thinking about Grandmother, Elmer slipped out the back door. I never heard a thing except the Carryall starting up. Unbeknownst to me, Daddy had gone looking for Ted Reed. He stopped the van in front of Ted's house and asked him to come out. "I would like to talk with you," he said. But Ted Reed would not come out of the house. Daddy screamed, "The next time you sick your mean dog on me or my kids, I am going to kill you."

Ted hollered back: "You ort to see what your boy did to my dog's head. Damn you. I am just going to kill you right now."

Just as Elmer's hands opened the gate, Sirus Alls laid his hand on Daddy's shoulder. "Now Elmer, Ted Reed just ain't worth killing. If anyone else ever gets bit by that mean dog, I am personally going to come down here and kill that mean dog for you. You too, Ted, if you make one step toward getting in my way." Mr. Alls had just gotten off from the midnight shift at the power plant and had come out of his house to check on all of the commotion.

The next day, the big mean dog was on a sturdy chain. He stayed on the chain, too. Ted knew that Mr. Alls was a quiet man and never bothered anyone. But that said, if he told you he was going to hit you in the nose, you might as well go on and get your handkerchief out.

Now Old Elmer did have his faults, but he loved us kids. Why, he would even take a chance that Ted Reed would sick that mean dog on him. As for me, that Raleigh Salve pulled me through again. I had a very big bruise and four little tooth wounds, but it was worth it all to hear Sirus Alls brag on my daddy. He said, "I sure would not have wanted to be Ted Reed that night."

Another thing here. After careful thought, I think that I most likely did more damage to my leg hitting the dog over the head with the Double Cola bottle. Those bottles were very big and hard. The old dog did have a-holt of my leg, but hitting him on the head while he was biting just might have drove his teeth deeper into my leg.

Here is something else to think about. I just pitched the 12-gauge up on the picnic table outside. If I had put it back in the corner, Daddy just might have taken it with him to visit Ted Reed. One just never knows what might have been.

The First Time Me and Elmer Went Out Drinking

Riding around and drinking beer on weekends is something about all redneck males do. Age has nothing to do with this at all. It is part of the sacred male Appalachian tradition that is bred into us right from the start. I say male, because there is no age limit on going out drinking, and I've never seen but a few females take part. Riding around and drinking beer is just part of us or a ritual or something. It is just important. It is, I am telling you.

This falls into the same genre as going to Mountain Lake on the afternoon of the first snowfall. You just got to see who has made it up the hill and who hasn't. In years past, I have been known to set around on the side of the road up there on Mountain Lake with a case of warm Blue Ribbon beer stacked up in a small snowdrift waiting for the beer to cool, just talking away with the other men who came up for the afternoon. Doing this is kind of like knowing that you must sign a petition and support the movement to make the first day of trout season a national holiday. It is as natural and normal as cutting firewood or picking up rocks from out of the garden. All solid upstanding redneck males do these things. They do. I know. I am one.

My indoctrination into this Appalachian Manhood Ritual (the AMR, as I like call it) came at an early age. It was before I could even talk or walk. I may not have even grown any teeth yet, either. It started even before I could remember. I was riding around drinking with my father. I am sure that he just wanted me to learn how to do this the correct way. So it was; I was imprinted, sort of like geese who decide the first thing they see is their mother.

Mom tells me that one day Daddy had the urge to ride around and drink beer. Being a good father, he wanted to take me with him. Mom fixed me up a diaper bag. She put in some butt-washers, a half dozen diapers and a six-pack of little 5-ounce baby milk bottles. Elmer and I were off. Elmer would drink himself a can of good, cold Blue Ribbon beer, and I would suck down a good, cold bottle of milk. When Elmer pitched his empty beer can out the window, I flipped (I may be proud, but I know I couldn't pitch then) my empty milk bottle out that same window.

When we got home, Momma asked Daddy, "Where are the little baby bottles?" And Daddy just smiled. True story. Well, you got to learn this stuff somewhere. Me? I learned it from one of the best, and I grew to be one of the best!

Uncle Fred and the
Trip to the Curb Grill

This story was told to me by Uncle Fred more than 50 years ago. We were sitting on the riverbank by the old bus. I think that we were deer hunting or something. Leastways, he might have been; I was just sent to keep watch on him. There was a quart Kerr fruit jar of white lightning setting on an old truck tire, and we were smoking some of those unknown varieties of cigarettes that he was famous for. He had driven up from Richmond for one of the one or two long visits he made each year. When Fred asked me about the Curb Grill and if people still went up there much, I told him it ceased to exist after the new road was built.

He said, "Well, it's probably a good thing that no one goes up there anymore. It was kind of a rough place." He added that one weekend before the War, he had driven up for a visit and rather than go to Grandmother's house first, he went to the Curb Grill "to see who was out and about." As he pulled into the little parking lot, he saw a man being choked to death by another man. He explained to me that, "It wasn't none of my business, so I just went on and parked my new Ford."

This man was being choked with the hose from a gas pump. "Rough stuff went on up there, mighty rough," he said. "If you wanted your bill braded, there was always someone there more than willing to help you out."

It seems like all coal-miner hangouts were right rough. As Fred walked by and looked down at the man being choked, he realized it was his brother, Elmer. Yes, his brother and my future father was the one being strangled!

"Well, now it was some of my business," Fred said. He reached his hand into his pocket and took out his trusty 32 Owl Head Pistol and touched it to the ear of the man who was choking Dad. Fred then said, "Now, don't you think that Elmer is just about dead enough?"

He didn't tell me what happened next. I guess the man turned Daddy loose. I'm here, am I not?

I, too, went to the Curb Grill, and I, too, had an interesting experience. It was the year that Audie Murphy was killed in an airplane crash on Brush Mountain. I was working at Mick or Mack Grocery Store at the time, but it was my day off. I had re-baited my trot lines and fished until my arm was getting tired. It was too hot to squirrel hunt that summer; the gnats in the woods would have worried a fellow to death. So I decided that I would drive out to the top of Brush Mountain to see if I could find the place where Audie Murphy's airplane had crashed.

When I drove up new route 460 and turned off on old 460 at the top of the mountain — I had not been that way in years — I rounded the turn and there stood the Curb Grill. Right at this minute I got hungry, so I thought I'd just eat at the Curb Grill as I had numerous times in the past. I parked my old blue Chevrolet pickup, most likely in the same parking space that Uncle Fred had used. My truck was the only car in the small lot. I walked in and sat down. There was still seating for four average people like me or six like you.

No one ever came to take my order, so I walked over to the door leading to the kitchen and knocked. A very old skinny lady came out. She had a newly lit Pall Mall cigarette sticking out from between her teeth and her head turned sideways to keep the smoke from burning her eyes. I have to admit I was just a little suspicious. You see, she still had on her bathrobe. I said, "I would like to order lunch." She just went back into the kitchen. I waited, and in just a little while she came back with two slices of toast on a little plate.

She sat down across from me in the little booth and quietly slid the toast in my direction. Without taking the Pall Mall from her mouth she said, "You know, we have been closed for three years." I jumped up and apologized for just walking into what was now this old lady's house. She patted me on the hand and insisted it was okay. "People come up here all the time and walk in and sit down." She recalled that this was once a hopping place, but that was before they built the new road. All the people just left, she said. I got up and left, too. I guess progress does come at a price. But the main thing here is that I, too, have a story about the Curb Grill. My last trip may not have been good as Daddy's was, but that's okay.

After writing this story, I decided to drive up to the Curb Grill one more time. There isn't anything left but the concrete foundation and pieces of the roof pillars. Another piece of local history is just that — History. Maybe that, too, is a reason for me to try record these short stories? Much of my father's past is just gone.

Yes, I Too Was a Coal Miner

A lot of people do not know that many of the hillsides in Montgomery County, VA, were pocked with coal mines. If it were not for the new growth of trees, the hills would look like I did after the chicken pox. Some of the mines were very large operations, like the Big Vein in McCoy, the Red Star in Parrott and another big one in Merrimac. Even today you can see the remnants of all three. Then there was the Slusher Mine on the north end of Blacksburg. Virginia Tech got its coal there before the railroad came to town. Finally, there were numerous small, nameless mines all over the mountains along Tom's Creek and up in Poverty.

I have always speculated, and I do not know this for a fact, that Poverty got its name from the poor coalminers eking out a living in Brush Mountain and living in rundown clapboard houses with cracks big enough for the snow to blow in and cold enough that it did not melt. My uncles showed me the last of these houses near the foot of Brush Mountain. Miners worked all winter for low pay called "company scrip," company money to be spent at the company store. In warmer months when the demand for coal dropped, everyone slaved in little gardens or worked their hearts out in corn, bean or tomato patches, canning up anything that ran slow, had no big briars, or did not bite first.

One of my first fulltime jobs — I had just turned 13 years old — was working in "Little Vein Mine" run by my uncles. I was big for my age. Why did they open a mine? All of the men were unemployed at the time. The economy was in a slump and they needed money, so they went back to what they knew. "If you can't find a job, you just got to make one," Uncle Nelson would say. The Lytton men were not always the best educated, but they were smart and had grit. They would work!

The mine was up in the Tom's Creek area, very near Jefferson National Forest. Everyone said that it was the same coal seam that ran all the way down to the old mine on Poverty Creek. My uncles' mine had been worked before, but by whom I cannot recall. In good weather, there was a pretty good dirt road. When it rained it was almost impossible to drive, so we either walked in or did not work. The big red oaks covered and shaded the road. When the sun shone through the trees, it made tiger-like stripes on the road. There was a little creek or branch near the front of the mine. In the blazing summer heat, along with the earthy smell of the coal pile, you could smell the drying woods and the scent of scrub pines and rotten oak leaves. Mix that with the sound of that little spring branch — well, I liked it.

When it rained, the smell was of rotting oak leaves, and the coal pile took on an odor of sulphur. (I just like that spelling better than sulfur.) I liked everything there was about this mine. Even today, I can walk through the woods and get a smell of the leaves and see myself back there with my head under the water, drinking my fill from the little branch. Back then there was no Guardia to worry about or contaminants in the water. Either that or some of our daily alcohol-drinking had pickled them Guardia. Well, anyway, we never got sick from drinking from the spring branch.

The mine was small, but I could stand up in most places. In some little veins, the seam of coal was very narrow and the over burden of coal rock was so hard to remove that the mines were not very high. A miner had to lie on his belly to dig the coal and stand on his knees to load it. We could stand up in places. By 13 I was nearly six feet tall, so I had to walk bent over in the mine. But I wasn't on my knees like some of the miners that Shorty and Nelson talked about.

This particular vein of coal ran flat or straight back into the mountain. At no time did it turn downward. It was easy digging, easy to get at and easy to get out. At least that is what my uncles kept saying. I did not see it that way. This was damned hard work! You see, I was tough, real tough — but not tough enough in the beginning. My job was not digging coal, but loading it and pushing it. I would push the coal car or hopper back into the mountain. It took every bit of strength I had to get the rascal moving. As soon as you started into the darkness, you always set a number of small rocks on the rail. (I will tell you in a minute how this braking system worked most of the time.) Once you got it going you just needed to keep a pretty steady push on it and follow it back into the mountain. After a while the old car ran into a small pile of coal and rock, where it would stop.

Once my eyes adjusted to darkness and I got my lamp adjusted, I would pick up an old well-worn Number 8 coal shovel and start loading the freshly dug coal and rock into the hopper car. The big lumps I picked up by hand, then broke them up with a sledgehammer and pitched them into the hopper. When it was full, I was supposed to roll the car out the same way that I brought it in. Bringing it in was not that easy. Empty, I bet the little coal hopper weighed at least 1,000 pounds or more. Taking it out was a truly a man-size job; in the beginning, it was a real two-man job. To get the thing moving, you needed to put your shoulder on the car as low as you could, hook your hand on the bottom, and get your legs even and together. Your knees needed to be bent and right up near your chin. Then you would hook you toes onto a crosstie and push with all the energy you could find.

In the beginning, I could feel veins in my head swell up and hear the muscles in my back strain. My thigh muscles would just quiver. Somehow, each and every time, it would slowly start to roll. Going out you had to push harder and steadier than you did coming in, all the time searching with your feet for crossties, then hooking the balls of your feet and toes to them. You went no more than a 100 yards under the mountain, but in a strain it felt more like a mile!

In most mines the moving of coal cars in and out was done with a pony, a mule or a donkey. Not here: it was done by a Charles — that was me. You see, this was a poor mine, one just scraping by. They could not afford a mule or a pony.

Once you got the car up to a certain speed, you needed to be very careful. If it got to going too fast, you could not stop the damn thing. You see there was a tipple, at least that is what they called it. I thought it looked more like a place to either get a leg cut off or your body broke or even killed. The wooden tipple structure was built about 30 or 40 feet out over the valley at a height of about 20 feet. And, in truth, it did resemble a dead-end, wooden train bridge. There was no walkway either. So here I am coming out of the mountain with a carload of coal, truly a ton of coal, often more. As soon as you got to where you could get around this runaway load of coal, you took to running to get in front of the coal hopper. You had to see if your little coal rocks were still on the rails. If they were not, "You better damn well get some more on the rail and be quick about it." These were Shorty's exact words, and for once he was not fooling. You see, each time the coal hopper hit and crushed one of these rocks it slowed down some. You could not use a big rock. The coal hopper's wheels would just knock it off. They had to be small enough to have the hopper crush them.

If you had put enough on the rail and used rocks of the right size, you could pretty much stop the car where you wanted it. As the coal pile got bigger, the farther out on the tipple you needed to take the coal car. I did not like that, but as the summer moved on I could run the hopper right to the end of the tipple then stop the thing on a dime. I could run the narrow rails like a tom cat. All in a very fast motion, I could hold onto the side of the rolling coal car, then swing around the side and hit the dump lever with my foot. I swelled with pride doing this. Yes, I was tough, strong, and coordinated, but still rather rotund. I liked to think of myself as right manly developed.

I would jump down to the ground and start sorting and screening. The shale and coal rock needed to be sorted from the good coal. At first, it all looked like the same thing to me. In the evening before we left for the day Shorty, Nelson and Gibb would check over the sorted coal pile. Before long, I was as good as they were at coal sorting.

The coal also had to be cleaned and graded by size, which was called "screening." I would take a very large shovel and pitch the coal up on to a screen separator, which sorted it by size and removed the dirt. There were three screens. First you pitched the coal up on the screen with smallest holes. You then took what was rolled to the bottom of the screen and pitched it up the next size screen. The process was repeated for the third screen. In the end you had three uniform piles of clean coal for sale: pea, nut, and lump were the sizes. I had to keep at least one pickup load of pea, nut and lump on hand at all times. If I needed more of the pea or nut size, I took a sledgehammer and broke up larger pieces of the lump coal.

Every day someone would drive up and want to buy a pickup truckload of coal. Often men would show up with larger trucks wanting two or three tons. The piles of cleaned, screened coal had to be ready. I found nothing easy around the mine, nothing. I would pitch the coal on the truck, and sooner or later one of the men would say, "Well, that is about a half a ton or that is a load." I would just go back to work.

Sometimes people called Uncle Nelson "Horse." I am telling you that he was just that: he was as strong as any horse. When I took what he called "a number eight scoop" and pitched the coal to the top of the screen for cleaning, he told me that was the wrong way. "You pitch the coal on to the bottom of the screen with enough force to roll it all the way to the top. This way, when it falls to the ground it has been run over the screen two times."

Now, I am telling you, it takes a horse to do this very long. Nelson, "The Horse," could do it as long as there was coal to clean and separate. He just laughed at the job! Mod Snider said that Uncle Nelson so strong because he was a DeHeart - Lytton cross.

Sometimes people wanted coal hauled to their house. Once I would get a truckload sorted, it was loaded onto Uncle Shorty's pickup truck. Now that little truck was something else. A green, 1950 (or thereabout) one-ton International with a three-speed shift in the floor, it wouldn't go much over 50 miles per hour anywhere. You could have dropped it off Lovers Leap, and it still would not have gone more than 50 miles an hour. But, put a little load on it, and it would go anywhere. The steeper the hill, the more the old truck liked it. She was tough as the men that loaded her. The old truck had to be. I was also the coal delivery man, or boy, as the case may be. As I told you earlier, I was big for my age.

When I would drive a truckload out of the mountain to people's houses, the buyers would meet me and tell me what do with the coal. My instructions were simple: "Get the money before you unload a lump of coal. Count it and put it in your pocket. If you lose it, do not come back. Just send the truck."

Sometimes men would meet me and tell me where to pile it up or show me the doorway to shovel it into the basement. If women met me, they would make me go down into the basement and make sure the coal was piled up and out of the walkway. Men were not so particular. I would jump back into the truck and head back to the mine, always stopping at Nutter's Store to get two or three Double Colas. They were the first 16-ounce bottles of pop on the market. If the store was sold out, I would opt for RC Cola, since they were the next biggest ones. I always had them drunk by the time I got to the mine and had to start pushing the hopper again. Deep in the mine, I was always greeted with a very large pile of coal to be loaded and moved out of the mountain.

Coal mining, like anything else that had true-blue Appalachian American men involved, included alcohol. Often you hear sociologists talk about the role that alcohol played in Appalachia. They do not have a clue. I tend to think of sociologists as people who pronounce Appalachia as Apple-ate-ya, not Appa-latcha. The first pronunciation is reserved for those not living around here; those who just talk about our mountains and have never once picked up a Number 8 coal scoop. Often they've never even seen them mountains about which they try to talk. They have only read about this world, and never once lived it. The other is for the men and women that live here. Work here. Understand here. Those of us from Appalachia know the place to be warm, pretty and full of wonderful people.

Yes, there is a difference, a mountain of difference. There was not a day in the mountains that we did not drink alcohol in one fashion or another. There was always a Mason jar in the creek with a rock setting on the lid. Cool shine is the best kind. Sometimes, Blue Ribbon beer was there in the creek, too. Someone was always coming to buy a pickup load of coal. They had a jug, too. Everyone would walk back into the cool of the mine and talk. Many of these men had been miners in their youth. I wondered if their mining careers had started off as a car pusher like mine. I also wondered if I was always to be a coal miner. While I was wondering, the bottle always got set down near me. I'd take a drink, but not a big one. I did not want to start coughing and sputtering like I had seen the men do when they took a big drink. When they talked and rolled up a cigarette, I would too, and we enjoyed the cool of the mine. Sooner or later someone would say, "Don't you think you just ort to load the coal car?"

Lunch was a treat! I almost always had cold biscuits left over from breakfast, a large tomato from the garden, a can or two of Vienna sausages, a can or two of sardines, and any other breakfast leftovers. One favorite was a fried bologna sandwich. Just like my uncles, I would go to the spring branch and draw out a good cool beer or Double Cola. The beer was the kind that needed an opener. I can still see the beer opener tied on long shoestring. "By jingos," Gilbert would say, "you don't want to lose the church-key, now do you?" By jingos was about as rough-talking as Gilbert ever got. I think those beers were better than the pop-top kind. At least the memory is better.

After a few weeks of steady learning, my tolerance to alcohol was growing. I could gulp down bootleg with my uncles, even if I still coughed and gagged, and they still laughed at me. I would drink a can or two of beer whenever the chance came. I learned to gulp down the stuff, not drink it slowly. We drank up all kinds of cheap wine. If customers came with booze, we drank up what they had. Shorty would never let me drive the truck to deliver coal if anyone had been around with any liquor. I guess he knew I was taking a little nip or two now and again.

Once in awhile, after a coal delivery I had to make a run to the bootleggers' for them. It was easy: you just go to one of the bootleggers' houses. Several of them had moonshine, and they were right close to the mine. Other bootleggers had "bottle and bond" as they called it. This store-bought liquor was purchased at the liquor store in Christiansburg and carried to the mine side of the county for resale. It was a little more costly, but it was close and right handy, too. All you had to do was drive up, go to the front door of the house and announce that Shorty, Nelson or Gilbert "want a bottle or two of hooch." Hand them the money, and they gave you the hooch. Pretty simple, so simple even a boy could do it.

I remember one time I had come back to the mine and everyone was setting around waiting for me to return. I pulled out the quart jar of bootleg, and they started passing it around. Then, a man that I did not know jumped up and ran to the creek for a drink of water. Whatever it was they were drinking was pretty strong. He coughed and sputtered just like me. The others did not laugh at him, though. He lay down in the edge of the stream and took a long, steady big drink of good cool water. He was trying to cool off the bootleg. He then jumped up, and stood right still for a second, with a funny look on his face. He announced that he had "swallowed a lizard" and said that he could "feel him wiggling around" in his stomach. Then he quietly said, "He's quit wigglin' now." After that, none of us drank straight out of the creek anymore. We all found us a can or jar to use as a dipper. I always use a Vienna sausage can myself.

Times do change, don't they? Every time I think about going to Poff's Store I have to chuckle. Today, if we were to make this trip and make the request for dynamite and caps as we did every week back then, an anti-terrorist group would swoop down on us, and put us in the jail and throw away the key.

Every once in a while we needed dynamite for blasting coal, so we went to Poff's Store in the community of Vicker. Now this was a store if there ever was one! You could get anything you ever wanted at Poff's — food, clothes, mining tools, shoes and dynamite.

To get the dynamite, you went to the counter and just announced, "I need to get some dynamite." That was all there was to it. There were no papers to fill out, no explanations, nothing. The man behind the counter would hand you a key to the small cinderblock building in back of the store. It looked kind of like a larger root cellar. You went out back, picked up all you could afford, went back in and paid for it. We would roll each stick in dry newspaper to keep the sticks well formed. We bought blasting caps, too, which we stored in one-gallon Mason jars. You wanted to keep them undamaged and dry.

When it came time to blast coal, I would set me out a stick of dynamite to use as an example. Then I would role 12 exact replicas of the real stick. There were called "dummies." Dummies were filled with bright orange clay and used as packing in holes. Nelson, now he was the dynamite man! He would let me help drill the holes. We had a 1 ½-inch manual twist drill eight feet long, just like the one used in a carpenter's shop, only larger. Uncle Nelson would chip out a spot and hold the drill tip in place while I cranked it. I held the big wooden handle against my stomach and started turning the bit with both hands. When I would give out, old Horse would start turning. Big beads of sweat would come up on him and leave streaks of clean on his face. Then it would be my turn again. After a while, we had a six-foot hole in the base of the coal seam. Sometimes we made two or three holes.

This was one time when no one was drinking any alcohol. Everyone was as stone-cold sober as the local Holy Roller preacher. You took two sticks of dynamite, one blasting cap, all of the clay-packed dummies, a 200- foot insulated wire, and the pickup truck battery and tamp rod back into the mine. While the yellow wire was being uncoiled, Nelson and me went to work. Well, Nelson placed the dynamite, and I just held my carbide light. Nelson would carefully mush up one end of a stick of dynamite and push a blasting cap deep into it, then wrap three or four coils of blasting cap wire around the dynamite real tight. Carefully he put the blasting cap end in the hole. Using the tamp stick, he pushed the dynamite to the bottom of the hole. Next, he pushed the second stick into the hole. Then he started pushing the clay dummies in, tamping them firmly. Once that hole was full of dynamite and clay, we would move to the next hole.

Then we real carefully looked for all the tools and put them in the coal hopper and pushed it out. The dynamite wires were connected. Nelson would hook one wire to a battery post with a pair of vice grips and hold the second wire to the other post. The ground would shake. And the strong-smelling sulphur smoke would always beat Nelson out of the mine. I never got used to the smell of the smoke or the feeling of fear going back in after a blast. My uncles would tell me: "Sometime

we will go to West Virginia and watch them shoot a big mine."
Sometimes they would talk about the Great Valley Mine and
how the mountain would rumble and everything would shake.
Yeah, sounds like real fun, don't it?

I think that my uncles did like every aspect of mining.
In some ways, they lived for it. The taste of coal gets a holt of
you. It might have been that family thing, since they had all
spent so much of their youth mining. Just watching Nelson
load dynamite into the hole with me standing beside him with
the carbide lamp on my hat was enough to insure that the line
of Lytton miners stopped with them. I am right sure they knew
what they were doing, but it still was no place for a boy. I was
big for my age, but at times like these, I was just a boy still.

Another mine job that got your attention and kept it was
cutting mining timbers. Shorty had a David Bradley chainsaw.
It was one of the old ones. To me, the bar looked to be 36
inches long, and the total weight of the saw was about 50 or 60
pounds. It took a real man to use this thing. The engine could
be adjusted to a vertical position, not sideways like the ones
today. Why, the bar even had an attachment for it to convert
to a two-man saw. Yes sir, no boys played with that thing. It
was big, but everyone said that it was a lot better than cutting
with a crosscut saw.

Who has that old saw, or has it just vanished? The only
bigger saw known to man was the Maul, or something like that,
that Chuck Shorter had. I did not even like the sound of that
thing. Both were old gear-driven machines with chains that

were again as big as the ones you see today.

Mining timbers are short timbers, four to five, sometimes as much as six feet long and from six to ten inches in diameter. We cut them right in front of the mine. They were mostly made of white and red oak, very strong and readily available. No one but me seemed to notice that they were pretty damned heavy. That did not seem to bother anyone but me. My job was to carry them from where we cut them up the side of the hill to the mine entrance. I loaded them into the waiting coal car, which now became a timber-moving car. Every few days, as the mine grew deeper, new mine timbers had to be set. This, too, was a task for sober men with good eyes for what they were doing. One slip of the jack, and someone was going to get hurt! These timbers I speak of had to be cut to the exact length and be set about every ten feet or so. Their function was holding up the mountain while you dug and shot coal.

I always heard about cave-ins and rocks falling from the ceiling and how you could be either killed or trapped or both. Being killed and trapped truly got my attention. I would roll the coal car back into the mountain. A VERY big jack with a large block of wood on the top was placed against the ceiling, and pressure was put on it. One of the timbers that had just been cut was placed beside the jack. Sometimes a small wooden wedge was hammered in between the timber and the mine ceiling. Once in a while, you could hear the mountain groan during this process. Maybe I ain't going to work in the mines fulltime forever.

I just never got used to things like the sound of the mountain groaning and the nonstop sweating. I mean like sweating all of the time. You see, there are two kinds of sweating, and they don't really have much in common except where the sweat comes from. That is because everything was pure work. The out-of-the-mine sweat came from unloading the coal car, sorting coal from rock and loading coal into a pickup truck with a big square shovel. Or sweat from being sent to carry in more timbers. Or sweat from screening a pickup load of coal for a customer. That was a very hot sweat.

Now inside the mine was a very different kind of sweat. It is a kind of cold sweat. I would work up a sweat loading the coal hopper, carrying rails and little ties or drilling shooting holes. I would sweat a lot when pushing the car out of the mine. The inside sweat would just kind of bake off of you when you got to the sunlight. Then your body started over making the other kind of sweat. I do not think there was one easy job in that Little Vein Mine.

I got to where I was very strong; I could bring that coal car out of the mine like a freight train passing a hobo. I could run it to the very end of the tipple and stop it on a dime. I did not need a catwalk to get out onto the tipple. I could balance on the rail while I pushed the car like a wild man and hit the dump lever and never miss a beat. I could sort coal and make deliveries. I could load mine timbers, drag in rails and six-foot crossties for the small railroad track always begin expanded back in the dark mine. I got used to the smell and taste of hard liquor. I even got used to taking a bath every day on the creek bank, watching black men turn back into white men. I even got used to Uncle Nelson telling me once or twice a day, "Why boy, if I was as big and strong as you, I would hunt every pick-and-shovel job in the county."

Never once did they say get a real job or finish high school. No, just hunt for low-paying, hard-work jobs. I think that was about what they knew. The way these men worked, I bet they would have all been good pick-and-shovel men. They were flat out tough, could drink like fish and dig like moles. But one thing that shook me was the sounds the mountain made; no sir I never could get used to it.

What a summer!! What an adventure!! I may not have climbed a mountain or swum in an ocean, but my first experience right up close with mining was a real-time adventure. Today, when I tell people about my first real job, they look at me like I am a lost ball in the high weeds. I don't think they know what it takes to have two kinds of sweat making coal streaks on your face. Today, I have my name chiseled on a Coal Miners' Monument on Tom's Creek. My name is right beside Oakley "Shorty" Lytton and Robert N. Lytton. It is not too far from Gilbert Hilton's name. Yes, once upon a time I was a real honest to goodness coal miner.

Sometime later, Chuck, Terry and me were in Wake Forest and went in the little mine there that Barney Montgomery, John Dewease and Snake Page were working. We walked down into mine about 1,000 feet. With my old carbide lamp, I could only see the whites of the men's eyes. But my ears were ok. I will remember to my dying day what Barney Montgomery said to us: "Mining, she is a hard way to serve the Lord." For once in my life, I truly understood what he meant to say. I think the mine is an unforgiving way to make a living and a hard mistress. I truly know very little about mining. I was just a boy and just saw some of it. But I will never forget it, either.

The Big Coal Pile in McCoy and My Little One

Now I would like to step away from the little mine on Tom's Creek and move down to McCoy, Virginia, to the Big Vein mine. This was no more than 10 or 12 miles west of my little vein. When I was a boy, the Big Vein had not been worked in more than 25 years. At the time the mine closed, they were working deep under New River and pumping water out 24 hours a day just to stay ahead of the incoming water. There was an equally big mine on the Bell Springs side of the river. Daddy, Shorty and Nelson speculated that it was the same vein. It just happened to run under the river. I have no idea if this is true.

There was a fire at the Big Vein. From what I gather it was started by spontaneous combustion. I do not know exactly when. It burned the pile above ground and deep underground for years. The subsequent explosion and cave-in killed 20 or 30 fine, hard-working men. The economy of a small Appalachian Community died with the mine, too. If you want to know more about this you will need to track down Miss Queen. She kept up with everything and knew about everybody. When I was a little boy, in early September when the fog was thick and white, I can remember standing at the road waiting on the school bus and smelling a trace of the rotten-egg smell of the fire more than ten miles away. It had to be damp for the smell to reach all the way to River Ridge, but it did. The fire burned for more than 20 years and burned out by 1962. But the smell still drifted on the fog. It was so common that no one ever even mentioned it.

Back in 1970, me and my trusty 1964 Chevy pickup graveled the driveway at Mom and Dad's house and the road to the cabin with burnt cinders from the old Big Vein Mine. Lots of people did this, and few even asked how the cinders got there or why. About everybody just loaded them up and hauled them away.

Now, here is what I want to tell you. There in McCoy, on the next ridge over, there was pile of coal dirt as big as a large mountain. The fire never touched this pile. Truly — I am guessing here — there were four or five or ten million tons or more of coal dirt. Oak Sheppard's fulltime job was hauling this coal dirt to the Webster Brick Plant in Salem. There it was ground into pieces about the size of black pepper, burned up and made into bricks and cinderblocks to build houses. The coal rock and shale was not separated out. Everything was ground and pulverized then burned in the brick furnaces.

Mr. Sheppard had three of the biggest International tandem dump trucks that I had ever seen. Big blue ones they were. You could see one of these trucks going up or down the road all of the time. You could hear them day or night. They would pass you in Price's Fork; one might almost blow you off the road in Christiansburg. You could pass them struggling back up Christiansburg Mountain. The more trips they made, the more money they earned. Another point of interest — or scary obstacle — was the McCoy to Prices Fork road itself. It was a hard-topped, one-lane racetrack for teens. There was plenty of room for one car. Two cars could easily pass, if they both let their right tires come off of the hard top to make room. When you met one of the Big Blue trucks, the driver of the car had to head for the ditch! Based on the size of the Big Blue Giants, I never saw anyone question the right of way and Oak never slowed down to ask. If you knew what was good for you, you just stayed the hell out of the way. On a good day, one truck could make three maybe even four trips to Roanoke.

The best place to watch all the stuff in action was Gilbert Hilton's front porch. His house was at the steepest part of the Sucker Snider Hill and about 30 or 40 feet from the road. You were close enough that you had to squint your eyes when the truck labored up the hill. If you didn't, the wind might blow coal dust in your eyes. No one talked when the trucks passed. You couldn't; they were too loud.

From the porch of Gilbert Hilton's house, you could see and hear them coming down the Bob Price Hill as fast as gravity, centrifugal force and other laws of physics would allow. They were trying build up as much momentum as the curved road would permit. It sounded like they were going to throw a rod or explode. Them diesel engines were screaming for mercy. It looked like the drivers were shifting gears every few seconds in an effort to keep the things clawing and scratching their way toward the top of the Sucker Snider Hill. Holy Macaroni, how I wanted to drive one of those things! The very thought of shifting those gears and racing to Salem as fast as the law and that diesel would allow just seemed like a great life. They always reminded me of great ships going across the sea, but I knew they weren't.

When I was about ten years old, I rode in the cab of one of Oak's Big Blue Giants. Johnny "The Fox" Stempson was the driver. He was only about ten years older than me, but he looked to be my senior by 30 years, with his red curly hair matted with coal dirt, and every crack and pore in his face filled with coal dust. I rode from Bobby Conner's Store to my house, a distance of no more than five miles, but the memory has lasted nearly 50 years.

Daddy and I were at Bobby Conner's Store when Fox stopped. When I asked if could ride with him to my house, he said yes while he looked at Daddy. The passenger seat was just big enough to set your lunch on, and that was about it. The truck was not made for passengers or any comfort. There was not one thing that resembled anything clean in it. Fox's eyes were white, and that was it.

We came down the Bob Price Hill as fast he could safely go, building up momentum for Sucker Snider Hill. When we made the sharp turn at the Esso Station, Johnny Fox mashed the gas pedal to the floorboard and held it there all the way to the Miss Albert's curve. The Blue Giant started to pick up speed, but not much. When we got about to Miss Albert's curve, the truck slowed down and the engine began to race. Johnny talked and smiled a lot, but I could not hear what he was saying. He also shifted gears a lot. When we got to the steep part of the hill, he was driving the truck with his knees on the steering wheel some of the time. Also some of the time, he had his arm run through the steering wheel. In each hand he had one of the two gear shifters. When we passed Gilbert Hilton's, we were moving no faster than a man could walk, but the big diesel kept up the charge, just like it could see the Lytton Cemetery up ahead and knew it could slow down then. Or maybe just die.

Every second or two, Johnny Fox would pump the clutch with his left leg. With each pump, he shifted one of the levers, first for the transmission and next the rear-end. This was the first I think that I had ever heard of double clutching. From Bobby's Store to my house I will bet you he shifted at least 25 times. But the gas pedal never left the floor more than two or three times. I think that there were five or six forward gears in the transmission and three or four gears in the rear-end. Johnny used each and every one of them gears shifters two or three times. Well, it looked like that to me. The Big Blue Giant lurched forward with each shift, and the engine wound up to the point it sounded like it would explode.

The truck's diesel engine bellowed like a hemmed up

giant bull. The torque created pulled the finder of the truck close to the front tire with each shift. It took a while to shift it all the way down into the lower gears. "She pulls good, don't she?" Johnny Fox screamed. The cab was so loud that I could not hear anything but the engine. My body kind of knew what was taking place by the truck's vibrations. I vibrated much like the empty Pepsi bottles jumping on the chain in the floorboard.

Once you got to the curve at the Lytton Cemetery, you had to start shifting your way back up to the faster or higher gears. The engine noise went way down, too. When we stopped, Johnny told Daddy that he had to "keep the oil boilt in old blue to get up the hill."

Elmer said, "Roll on, Big Blue." Elmer and all of the men liked to see them big trucks. I use that expression — "keep the oil boilt in it" — to this day every time I am hot and tired. Boilt means working hard, kind of like carrying out buckets of rocks in the hot August sun to fill the mud holes in Grandmother's driveway. That was the job I had missed when I took my ride with Johnny Fox. The word is boilt, not boiled.

For sure, truck-driving was the job for me! How or why would anyone ever want more? Now you just tell me that. Where do you sign up? It was more than just truck-driving and shifting gears all day long. I wanted the language and vocabulary that went with it. Just think about being able to say to people: "I had to get her into double low to get up the hill. If you are near to overloaded, you got to go plumb to the bottom of them gears, if you expect to get up that hill. If I can get it up to 12th gear by the time I am hitting the Linkous' Stretch, I won't shift much more for a while."

When I was a little boy, this was my dream job. Never know, someday I might even get a real good nickname like "Fox" or "Wildcat" or something! I always liked the nickname "T-Bone," but it just never seemed to come my way. And I never got to drive the big truck either.

Thinking back now, about the only clean spot on Johnny was his eyes. He worked six or seven days a week, as did all of the men. I bet that Oak Sheppard worked at that coal pile for 20 or more years. He never even made a dent in it. A person would have to haul coal dirt for 50 years if he expected to get rid of that McCoy coal pile.

Oak Sheppard and Punkin McCoy had the exact same job. Before we go on, his name was not Pumpkin, like the big orange vegetable. His nickname was a much-shortened Appalachian version of Pumpkin, just "Punkin" McCoy. Oak worked the big pile in McCoy, whereas Punkin worked the smaller mines in the area. There was no comparison to the volume of coal dirt at my little vein, or any of the little mines for that matter. But, the dirt had to go somewhere. It was kind of like a molehill in comparison. With good weather, Punkin could haul ours away in a week or less. I would then start up making him a brand new pile of coal dirt and sweat.

After a while, under the tipple, I would have a very large pile of coal rock, coal dirt and good coal, too. Sometimes there would be as much as 200 tons or more if you added all of my sweat in it. That was a lot of trips out of the mine with that small coal car.

Just out of the blue, Punkin McCoy would arrive. No one truly ever knew when he was coming. Punkin was his own man and his own boss, so he worked on his own schedule. Now Punkin's job, like Oak's was hauling coal dirt. Sometimes he would work every day, Monday through Saturday, and even on Sunday too. Every once in while, Punkin even drove all night long. Just like Shorty, Gilbert and Nelson, grown men must not ever take off a day. It is like they live to work. Uncle Nelson and Shorty both said, "The Depression made men that way. They were working just to keep their families alive, and not trying to make a living." There is a difference. For us, too, I reckon, each and every day we went to the mine that summer.

Gibb, who was older than my uncles and knew them when they were growing up, said: "These men had to raise themselves or they would not have got raised up at all. All that they ever knew was hard, backbreaking work and low pay."

Gilbert told me this more than once: "Harmie, don't do this for a living. You have it in your blood. Get yourself out of this mountain before it takes a-holt of you. Coal gets into your blood and takes a-holt with a strong hand, and you just don't seem to be able to walk away." I think his reference to "in your blood" was a reference to Great Uncle Bayard and my uncles. My mother's family were miners from Pennsylvania.

Punkin took the coal from the coal pile to the Webster Brick Plant in Salem. All of the little mines up and down Poverty and Tom's Creek kept him busy. When he came to the mine, he was driving a little front-end loader, smoothing out the humps and filling the tire ruts in the dirt road. This was needed to smooth the road enough to drive a heavily loaded dump truck out. He made about four trips a day or more. As soon as he had cleaned up the pile, he moved on to the next little mine, and the process just started over.

A Memory of Mining and One's Youth

Just a few days ago, I stopped by one of the local stores to talk with my fellow retired loafers. It is real hard work, but someone has got to do it. After two or three cups of real strong coffee, made fresh once, and three or four fresh hotdogs, conversation started to drift off to the old days. At 62 years old, I now recognize those old days too.

I have learned that the "old days" is where life was about as good as it could get. People that had the misfortune to die too early sure did miss out on a lot of fun and the good things that life has to offer, that's a pure fact. According to the stories, some of these people still are handily missed even today. Also, it is agreed that some others that should have gone on and died off earlier did not. They were talked about in a very gaudy and hasty manner.

Out of the blue, Mr. Leon Sherman, a most respected 80-year-old man from the community of Wake Forest said: "Me, Shorty and Woosie were a three-man loading team down in the Big Vein Coal Mine." (Woosie was one of Uncle Nelson's many nicknames.)

One time down in the Big Vein there was this spot where the coal vein had taken a funny turn. There was a high hump or high knuckle, as we called it, on the limestone floor that reached almost to the ceiling. The coal seam followed up over it and then back down the other side all the way to the floor. You often found these knuckles in the coal seam. Most miners would have taken all the coal to the top of the limestone knuckle and not bothered with the rest, because it was just too hard to get at. But not us. We were being paid by the number of coal cars we loaded. This coal was already kind of loose and gravelly. It was easy to dig, but hard to get at and even harder to get out.

The seam was more than four feet high at that spot, and the coal came loose very easily. Shorty was the smallest, so he crawled up and over the knuckle, broke the coal loose, dug it out and pitched it to the bottom of the knuckle. Once there was room, I crawled over the knuckle, too. I scooped the coal up and pitched it over the top of the knuckle to where it slid down the other side to the bottom. Woosie then scooped the coal into the waiting car. "Lytton, we was young, tough as they come and strong, and we did not give a thought to how hard this work was. Scooping up coal three times wasn't nothing for us." ["Lytton." Leon never once in my life has ever called me "Charles" I was always "Lytton" to him. .]

"Yes, we were all young and did not mind hard work. We would outwork men just for the fun of it and laugh the whole time. We just wanted to fill a car with coal as fast as we could and put our tipping tag on it and send it out of the mine. You know, Lytton, if I was a young man I would go back into them mines today. I would!

"The people were good to each other, and we watched out for each other. The mine bosses were good to work for, too. Summer or winter, the temperature was always the same down in there. You know it was never too hot or too cold, and that means alot. The pay was real good, too. Now, William Notaway, he worked in town on Public Work and made $2.00 or $3.00 per day. Loading coal, a good man could make $12.00 to $15.00 per day. That was awful good money back in the day.

"Oscar Noons one time was working a wide face and loaded 40 hoppers in one shift. A person could not do this every day, for there just wasn't that much coal. But that 40 hoppers just might be a record of something. Oscar might have made $40.00 or $50.00 that day. Hell that was more money than the President made," said Leon Sherman.

Wide-eyed Harris was setting there with us, and he asked Leon: "What about the mine explosions, cave-ins and the nonstop danger? I have gone down into mines a few times, and it always seemed like the mountain was closing in on me. I could not get it out of my mind that the ceiling might fall down on me."

"Well there were dangers and that was for sure," Leon answered. "Danger for sure!

"I can remember like it was just like it was yesterday. I was dragging down a new ground of freshly plowed sod, out behind where Buford's garage was. Back in them days, me and Daddy both sharecropped when we wasn't working in the mines. You had to make a nickel where you could find one. I had just given the horses a long breather, then just got Nell and Cleveland back into steady work, with a steady stream of sweat coming out of me. At the time, I am most likely no more than a mile or so from the mine. I can remember that day just as it happened."

Without any intention or reason, Leon's coal black eyes looked slightly up over my head and away from me. I do think that his mind was working its way back to that new ground and the day of the explosion.

"The ground just started to shake and move. I felt it. Them horses felt it, too. They jumped in their harness and twitched. I had no clue what had just happened. In a minute or two, it was over, and I went back to work. In a few hours, my daddy came walking up over the hill. Without saying a word, he simply untied the second pair of horses and started to dragging the field in front of me.

"Sometime before dark we started for home. He still never spoke one word. Not until Mother put supper on the table and asked what happened in the mine today did he speak. He said: 'There was an explosion in the mine; I think that someone dug into very big pocket of gas and something set it off. Some men got killed.'

" Number of men lost their lives that day. Daddy was

in the mine at the time of the explosion. He was working near the east entrance at the time. The explosion took place over near the west entrance. Daddy never got a scratch, but he was plenty shook up. I think we all were."

"Squirrel," Coldwell asked, "did you quit working the mines or go back to work after that?"

"Yes," Leon answered, "I cleaned up before supper, and after I ate I went back for my shift in the mine. Daddy, he came in the next morning too."

"Wasn't you afraid of another explosion or cave-in?"

"Me? I don't think so. You knew that a man might drill into another pocket of gas and set off another explosion, but I just did not think about it. A few men left the mine and went to looking for public work. But most just came on in to work their shift in the Big Vein.

"The mines were good to me. Lytton, if I was young and strong again I would go back to work in the mines tomorrow. The pay was fair, too."

A Head Like a River Jack

Daddy always said that I had a head that was harder than one of those yellow "River Jack" flint rocks. Can you say "Traumatic Brain Injury"? Well, the truth is I can't say Traumatic Brain Injury very well, but I do think I know exactly what it is. I have a lot of experience in this area. I have sort of been involved in a lifelong science project focusing on Traumatic Brain Injury. It is my own personal research. Oh boy, do I have the data to prove it! Let's start off by saying I don't think of myself as accident-prone. I think I am either unlucky or just in the right place at the wrong time to almost get myself killed over and over, and strong enough and lucky enough to live through it.

My first lucky learning experience occurred in the year of 1965. Mr. Mod Snider had the contract with Virginia Tech to haul coal from the railroad stop over on State Route 114 to the powerhouse on the Virginia Tech campus. He had three very large dump trucks. All you had to do was back the truck up under the tipple, which is a bridge-like structure. Once everything was lined up, you opened the railroad coal car's bottom door and the coal came streaming down through a funnel and into the truck. In the late spring, summer and early fall, it was an easy job. Very dirty and dusty, but easy. Since the coal was right wet, it just streamed from the railroad car. But the dust just stuck to you like glue. Within minutes, all you could see was the whites of my eyes, or the reds of my eyes, because the coal dirt irritated my eyes right at the start.

In the early spring and late fall, it was a hard job. Let me add in here that when the coal cars were loaded in West Virginia, they were soaked with water to keep the coal dirt from blowing off in transit. When the coal was heavy and wet, it would not slide out of the coal car and had to be pushed down into the truck. You could move a large volume of coal with one shove. The catch was, you had to be very careful not to let yourself get pushed down into the hopper-funnel with the coal. If you went down, most likely you would suffocate before anyone could get you out or even knew you were trapped. To make things even more interesting, most of the time you worked alone on the coal car, while the trucks were parked below. Drivers drove the trucks, and I loaded the trucks, and that was just the way it was.

The worst thing that ever happened to me was getting pulled into the bottom of the coal car and buried up to my neck. I could only take very little breaths. I was trapped for a minute or less at the very most. An empty dump truck was parked under the coal tipple. When the coal car's bottom bay door was opened, I just held on for all I was worth and coal streamed by me. I did not get covered up, but it was touch and go for a second or two. In today's world this would not be a job for a kid. But when I was 14, it was good job. I was big for my age, some even said strong, but I had no experience at anything. Developing some common sense takes a little time. Daddy said, "You got to learn to work somewhere. It might as well be in a coal car."

Now unloading these coal cars in the winter was very different story. I learned that for each and every coal car, it was truly like playing Russian roulette. In some of the coal cars there was a very thick, hard crust of ice and snow over the coal. Often this layer was so hard you could walk on it. When you opened the bottom dump doors, you had no clue how much of the coal went into the hopper below. There often was an ice bridge over the coal car.

I had to be very careful crawling out on the ice-covered coal cars. Sometimes when I started digging down toward the open door, the frozen coal would break loose, and me and the coal went rushing down. How or why I wasn't hurt, I will never know. Once I got to the bottom, I stood astraddle an open door. One time I had a ten-foot wall of coal break loose and hem me up against the other wall of coal behind me. I just stood there as coal rushed past me into an empty truck setting under the tipple. Again, I was not buried. I never got hurt once. At the time I just thought that it was funny. At 14 years old everything seems funny. All I thought about was payday and how quickly I could load 15 tons of coal into one of those giant trucks.

Well, the truth is, I did get hurt once. This time I was outside the coal car. The weather was horrible. Unloading coal went on every day no matter the weather. "Them college boys have got to be kept warm and dry," the truck drivers would say.

This day there was a few inches of frozen rain and snow on the ground. A train engine had delivered two or three coal cars the day before, and they had set on the tipple during the freezing rain and snow. The first car was very near the unloading area. The unloading doors in the belly of the coal car must be aligned with the hopper door on the tipple below. To do this you open the hopper on the tipple. One person stands on the ground, watches the coal car bay door and yells when the car and hopper are in alignment. Often a coal car is moved no more than a foot or so.

A lever used to make this final placement was a very simple machine with a long hickory handle and complicated-looking foot. You placed the foot under the wheel and pulled down on the handle to get the coal car to move forward about one inch.

Keep in mind everything is covered with a thick layer of ice, including the rails. I place the foot under the wheel and push down hard. I had done this many times before, but never with rails covered with ice. This day, I am standing over the handle to get more force on the lever. To be on the safe side, I should have been almost swinging under the handle pulling down. I am not. I am standing on top of the handle, pushing down with my arms on the sides of the railroad car.

The truth is, I am in one of the most dangerous places that I have ever been in my whole life and don't even know it. I push down with all my body weight. The coal car does not move. Its wheel is lifted about the thickness of cigarette paper. Now I cannot turn the handle loose. I am just stuck in a very dangerous place. In less than four or five seconds, my arms are fatigued, and I must do something and quickly. So, I think that the best thing for me to do is quickly swing under the handle and then turn it loose. I give it a good try, but I am a lot too slow. A 100-ton coal car can move faster than you think when it's propelled by gravity.

The handle of the lever flies up out of control and hits me between my nose and upper teeth. I am knocked out colder than one of Uncle Shorty's summertime watermelons. I am unconscious for no more than a few seconds, ten at the very most. I am just waking up good when Mod Snider comes running toward me. Mod says that he has seen it all and what in the hell was I trying to do, get killed or something? I lose no teeth, but they are loose. I have a very bad bloody nose, blood in my ears and a very bad headache. Mod says that the handle hit me and knocked me clear. "You could have been killed, and what in the hell would I tell Ruth then?" He also tells me to be more careful and not to get hurt anymore. In a short while, I go back to work.

We take shovels and scrape ice off the rails and spot the

coal car. I climb the coal car again. Life goes on, I guess. As I look back, I am just happy to be writing. For that matter I'm happy to be able to do lots of stuff. Some things I do very well; some I just can't do at all. Could this be a Traumatic Brain Injury? The next day I had two very back eyes and swelled face. My head hurt for a week. My teeth got tight again, and I took off eating anything I wanted.

And of course there are more examples of experimentation with Traumatic Brain Injury. Now, you may not believe this, but once upon a time I was a genuine high school track star. Could run like a fast deer — according to me, that is! I like to think of myself as very fast, not just regular fast. Truth is I never ran anything in my life but my mouth. Some say that I am still good at that.

We are at Dublin High School. Everyone is warming up for the track meet. Some are running around the track, while others are jumping over hurdles and pole-vaulting. Me and other not-so-fast people are getting limbered up for the shot putt competition. When it comes my turn, I give my 12 pounds a toss. It goes out about 35 or 40 feet.

Everything is to work from the right. What I mean is that you pitch the shot putt and step out of the circle to the right. The person in the field returning the shot putt throws it back to their right. In essence, all throwing is done on opposite sides of the pitching circle. All is going well, and it is now my turn. I make my throw and step out to the right. I am hit in the head by a 12-pound shot putt from about 35 feet away.

Yes, your thinking may be correct; this could explain why I am the way I am. It may go a long way, anyway. Well, what was I saying again? Oh yes, shot putt in Dublin. Now I remember well.

I scream like a wild cat: "Damn you, Donnie Price."

This should have at least knocked me out or maybe even killed me. I sure am glad it did not do the latter. I am here, and that is a good thing. I don't know exactly what happened next, but some said I was not seeing too good, though I was standing upright. I finished the track meet. Surely I must have won my event. If not, I think I should have — just on effort alone. By now a lot of people had gathered around.

Back to Dublin. Some want to know what happened; others want look at me or something. Some just want to rub my head.

When I get hit, the adult who comes over and looks at my head asks me, "Did it hurt?" I just kind of look at him like, "Well, yes."

To be honest I think that I heard it more than felt it. It sounded like a very loud noise in my head, my teeth hit together very hard, and I was a little woozy. Plus, the crowd gathering around made me nervous. So I just thumbed a ride a home to River Ridge, track uniform and all. River Ridge and the waters of the New River have a kind of healing power of their own.

The only lasting side effect from this is a kind of dip in

my head. It is really going to show off nicely when I finish going bald. If you were to rub my head, you would find a dent on top, though it is not as big as you might think. In the mornings after I shower, I just kind of lean over a little to sling the water off. I do not think that the dent is big enough to hold much water. Maybe it is only large enough for a small minnow to live in.

The only medical attention I received was that coach or volunteer looking at my head and asking me if it hurt. Today, I bet I would be sent to a hospital in an ambulance. Possibly I would be flown to a head research center in a helicopter or something. Now does this qualify me to say that I have had a Traumatic Brain Injury or a head as hard as a River Jack?

Dear reader, you have not read anything yet. This little essay starts out on my birthday — May 17, 1980. I have been told that coal miners in West Virginia have it in their contract that they get off from work on their birthday. Well on May 17, 1980, I wish it had been my day off, for on this day unbeknownst to me, I was about to put the River Jack or flint rock or Traumatic Brain Injury theory to a test once again in the worst kind of way. The effects I would wear for the rest of my life!

I was working on construction in the Radford Arsenal. My job for the day was jackhammering out an old set of concrete steps deep inside a building. The air compressor that powered the jackhammer could not go through the door. The hammer and air hoses had to be dragged probably 100 feet into the building and then up to the top of possibly as many as 30 steps. I was wringing wet with sweat, and I had not even started.   So I went back out and started up the air compressor and start jackhammering.

After a while, the hammer bit was dull from yesterday's work, and a sharper one needed to be installed. So, rather than walk back outside and down the steps to cut off the air compressor, I made a rather dumb decision: I turned the jackhammer over and put my foot between the cut-on lever and the hammer body. Another interesting part of this story is that the safety lock that held the bit in the hammer body had been broken before I started to work. Turning the hammer upside down sounded safe enough to me. I had done this more than once; it was quick and easy. I also did not have to walk out to the compressor and then climb back up the stairs.

Well, something went wrong. I took hold of the bit and turned over the hammer. In theory this should have worked. But it did not. When the hammer was straightened up and I started pulling on the bit, the hammer cut on. The drill bit shot out full force. I was pulling on it, and now the air pressure was pushing it, too. I held on somehow and kept it from hitting me right between the eyes or anything important.

I was hit full-force in the mouth. Six teeth were knocked clean out and my nose pushed over to the right side of my face. I walked down to the construction office where they looked at me and confirmed that I had been hurt. "Yes, you have been hurt," said the shift supervisor.

I just got up and walked to my truck. I was going to the

doctor. One of the construction company bosses asked where I was going. I said "I think I had better go on to the emergency room, don't you?"

One of the construction bosses did drive me to the emergency room in my truck. The attending doctor called an oral surgeon, who looked at me and said for me to sign some papers since I needed to go into surgery quickly. I signed, and I went. I was put under a local anesthesia. I could hear everything they said. One doctor said to another, "Why in the world this didn't kill him is beyond me." All the while, all I can do is lay there and go; ". . .ahhhh. . .ah. . .AH. "

Today, I have an eight-tooth bridge in the front of my mouth. It needs to be replaced again. This time it will cost more than $20,000. I do like cutting corners, but they come at a cost. Back to the question of "River Jack Flint" or "Traumatic Brain Injury"? I think both. Here is where I am coming from. I get my teeth knocked out, go into surgery for about two hours, then drive myself home to the river and mow the grass. I get up and go back to work the next day. The construction people never say a word, and I never say a word. You see, I needed the money.

One month later the dentist fits me with this new bridge and tells me to take off a few more days to get accustomed to the new appliance in my mouth. I answer "What? I only missed about six hours of work when they were knocked out." I was thinking, "I am moving to Rhode Island in a few weeks. I need the money." The dentist just looks at me and puts his note to my employers in his trash can. I just know he is thinking, "By damn, the folks on River Ridge are tough."

I never did say I was too smart, did I? Yes, I think my head is about as tough as one of those yellow flint rocks we all called River Jacks!

The Old Duck Hunt as I Was Told

I have repeated this story because there is more to tell. Terry Albert read the first version, and he wanted to add a few more paragraphs.

For years, I had heard this story told. Pappy told it over and over. My uncles did too, so I think that there is a lot of truth in it. Somewhere around 1930, I think, Elmer was helping someone who lived along the lower end of the Whitethorne Community with their duck hunting. For the life of me, I cannot put a name on the man in this story. I remember only that he lived near Cowan Siding. He either worked on the farm at Whitethorne or lived in one of the old company houses near Mr. Whit's or around the old hotel near the train station. I am working on remembering it. Anyway, Pappy said that this event took place on the Cowan Farm at Whitethorne, which is the present-day Virginia Tech Research Farm.

Daddy would gather up cornstalks in early fall and build a sturdy duck blind around a heavy bench, making it look like a real big corn shock with a room inside. Person X had a small "cannon gun," as Elmer called it. The big gun was mounted on the bench. When you loaded the thing and test shot it, on the ground you carefully marked the size of the pattern. In later stories told by Shorty, Lake, Nelson, and others, the gun took on the name a "Blunderbust." Since all of my uncles told about the same story in one way or another, there must be more than a grain of truth in it, don't you think?

Anyway, I have since seen examples of a gun like this on the Discovery Channel on television. It looked much like the one used by Elmer Fudd in TV cartoons. Today these large guns are outlawed, but there are many examples in museums.

When the ducks started to come in and feed in the cornfields, you would put out very small amounts of corn in a spot the exact size of the spread of the shot. The objective was to kill as many ducks as you could in one shot. You fed the ducks a little every day just about daylight, so that every morning they would come to the corn shock blind first to feed. One morning before daylight, Mr. Unknown Person loaded the big shotgun with old nails, bolts, small round rocks, pieces of old wire fencing and any other thing he could find. When the duck numbers were at their maximum around the blind, he fired the "Blunderbust," sometimes killing 30 or 40 ducks at one time. The next morning he started baiting the ducks again.

Uncle Lake told me that Mr. Flannigan had one of the big guns mounted on a flat-bottom boat. He hunted large numbers of ducks on New River using about the same method as Elmer, only he shot into the area where the ducks set on the water at night.

Back during the Great Depression, people ate what they could find and made money where they could. For a while they shipped salted ducks in wooden barrels all picked and cleaned for city people too lazy to hunt their own. Now how would you like to go to Kroger Store and pick out a nice cannon shot duck that had been packed in salt for who knows how long? Today, I lean a little more toward fresh-killed.

This form of hunting was legal back then. Later it became illegal, but "you've still got to eat," my uncles would insist. The government collected up all of the big old Blunderbust guns it could find. Those that managed not to be collected are still around. Today, almost all are museum pieces. As for me, I have never seen one in real life, but I would sure like to.

Here is an addition to this story that took me totally by surprise. Terry Albert and I are talking one afternoon at the Long Shop Service Center. "You know that story you told not long ago about the old duck hunts?" he said. "Well, here is a part that you did not know."

One of Terry's relatives lives in New York, and he sent a copy of a New York paper home to Miss Helen, who was Terry's grandmother. When this mailing occurred, I have no clue. This relative walked into a barbershop in New York. A few of his friends were already there and planning to go duck hunting. "Well, I sure hope you are as good at duck hunting as these people in the mountains of Virginia," one of them said, then passed Terry's relative a newspaper with a story about this duck hunt.

The picture was of Terry's relatives and the story was of killing a barrel full of duck with one of those big guns. The new article and picture had been run in one of the local papers and the story picked up in a New York newspaper. Even back in the old days the world was getting smaller!

Digging a Toilet Hole

As I sit and think about it, digging a new toilet hole is a pretty shitty thing. Have you ever done this? Some have never done this even once. Well, I am glad for you! You see, I have done this job two times; yes two times, start to finish. When I was younger, lots of people out in the country had outdoor toilets. Some of the better ones were called "privies," "johns" or "the seat of ease." Ours was just a plain old toilet.

There were negative sides to having an outdoor toilet. When it was cold and snowing you had to go outside and take a walk to get to it, day or night. After a while you trained yourself to only have to go to the toilet during the daytime, because it was truly a long walk on a cold dark night.

As a general rule, there were no lines like the lines to get to the modern-day bathroom. There were some advantages, too. For one, these toilets did not require any water for flushing, so it was good for the environment. There was no need to close the door, either; no one was coming through that part of the yard unless they, too, had the toilet on their mind.

I was sitting out there one fine early spring morning when a mother skunk came walking up out of the woods just past the sycamore tree, right through the fence straight to the toilet. She had three little baby skunks with her, no bigger than a cat-headed biscuit. The troop just stopped about 20 feet from the toilet and looked at me. She had a certain look on her face as if to say, "And you say we stink."

If I had wanted to, I could have squirrel-hunted from the toilet seat, too. Squirrels came from the woods to the big white oak beside the toilet. Yes, from a good, well-positioned toilet seat you could see nature.

I guess as I got older one of the main draws to the old toilet, other than the workings of Mother Nature, was Daddy's booze. You see, Daddy used the toilet as one of his main places to hide his booze. He had many hiding places, but at the toilet he could do two or three things with just one stop.

He would not bring his hard liquor into the house, no sir. If you hide your booze, no one will ever find out that you are drinking it. It was a proven fact, Elmer's research of course, that no one ever smelled it on your breath. It could be onions that you are smelling, he thought. Or say he stumbled — that was caused by something in the floor that tripped him. Or that kind of wobble in his walk most likely was him fixing to catch the flu, and that was what was making him right woozy. If his speech was a bit slurred, it was caused by a chicken bone caught in his throat from yesterday's supper or something.

Well, for me, it was a limitless supply of Distiller's Pride, a cheap bourbon. That was Daddy's drink of choice for the toilet. Other places he drank Old Kessler or Kentucky Gentleman. But in the toilet, he liked his Distiller's Pride. I could just slip out there before school and take a little drink to fortify myself for the day. On Sunday mornings when we were playing penny ante poker, I could have myself a little snort to give myself nerves of steel. Sometimes a little snort was good after mowing the grass, too. I reckon in reality I was practicing to follow in Daddy's and my uncles' footsteps. One Sunday, just before the weekly card game, I spied Chuck coming out of the toilet with a kind of red nose. He had found the Distillers Pride. "Well, shucks," I thought.

One morning Daddy took me for very short walk into the backyard. I was about 8 years old, I'm guessing. He explained another one of the facts of life to me, which was that someone had to dig a new toilet hole before the old one filled all the way to the top. He went on to explain that it was not going to be him. He had marked it out for me. He gave me a rounded-point shovel and a pick. I went to work and dug on the hole every day after school. The red clay soil was hard, and the flint rocks made it even tougher. The hole was down only 18 inches, and digging was very slow. Then one afternoon some older young men came to help me, saying: "Harmie, Pickle called us and asked us to dig a new toilet hole. He said the old one would be full and overflowing and covered with snow if he kept waiting for you. You are right slow."

I did not care for any of their sarcasm and the rough way they treated me. But so be it. I just wanted this job to be in the past tense. I learned that I could put up with a lot of mouth and their constant bullshit to get it done. It may sound funny, but 50 years later I can still think back to these three or four days with them and say to myself, "What characters!" One brother went on to kill himself, and the other went to prison for killing a man. Anyway, in a day or two they had the job done. There was a hole that went halfway to China or deeper, and not one person got shot, stabbed or murdered.

We tied a rope around the old toilet and pulled it over with the horse, dragging it to the new hole and setting it up. Before you knew it, we were back in the crapping business. Oh, damn! Oh, gee! Oh, hell! Oh, shit! The old toilet pit needed to be covered with dirt. This was a nasty little task for an eight-year-old to be charged with. Holy Macaroni! Today this job would give a child nightmares and have his parents sent to jail for child abuse, but not in 1959, no sir. No one had to tell me to start covering the old hole. I was faster than a cat with 32 helpers. I had the dirt flying and got this job in the past also. When it came to toilet-hole digging, it seemed like every job was a little worse than the one before.

Within a year, I found myself deep in a toilet pit yet again. This time I was at Uncle Shorty's house. I was starting to think that once you got the toilet hole filth on you, and once you somewhat mastered the sociological scarring of what you were doing, the stain and strain might just stay on you for life.

Well that stain must have been on me, since I was doing this twice, and I wasn't even ten years old yet.

We dug a hole more than halfway to China this time. Somewhere near Russia or down about six or seven feet, we started digging it in the shape of a light bulb. We made a little cave on both the left and right side. Shorty said there was lot of crapping going on around here, and he was going to take care of it once and for all. I think all that digging was just another form of work-related torture that Shorty and Elmer had dreamed up for part of my growing-up training. There is no way anybody could crap that much or need that much training.

After a few days, this giant of a hole was finally dug! Then we set about building a good-looking, comfortable two-seater toilet. There was one large hole for grownups and a right small one for children. You see you did not want a child to fall in. I often wondered if you did fall in, who was going to jump in after you. But I never asked. I was always afraid that this might be my job, too. When I was in the toilet, I just held onto the seat real tight. I did not want to make a miscue and go down! We also built a little smokestack in the middle to let the odor out the top. I do not think it ever worked very well. It most probably needed to be three or four times bigger. The smell around this toilet was not like flowers.

Toilet-hole digging will make a man out of you. I know. About once per day I think back to the good old days when putting an electric light out there in the toilet was a great home improvement project. Today, I like the little shiny handle on the commode and not having to wonder about falling in, worry about frostbite on my butt, or think about getting someone out.

I also wonder if I could just go back to taking a walk through the snow at midnight. I just wonder. The memory of snow and ice on the ground was bad, but having to wipe the snow from the seat and sit your bare butt down was really hard. I can remember having to shake the coal ashes out of the heat stoves and spread the ash on a narrow path so Mamaw could make her way to the outhouse. She had real bad arthritis, but she still had to go. Elmer and Shorty said that I needed to do this every day that there was any snow or ice on the ground.

Just Letting Time Pass

on the River

From the time I was big enough to know much, Daddy and Shorty would take me to the river to chop weeds out of the corn. I soon learned that June Tallent was right about Johnson grass: the only way to beat the stuff was to die and leave it for the next generation.

I thought that going to chop weeds was great. I got to sit on the horse's back, or Uncle Shorty would hold me as I sat on the two-footed cultivator plow. I preferred sitting on the horse. If you were sitting on the cultivator, when Old Fanny farted, you got the full effect. You could smell it right strongly. Bad ones you could even taste, so I knew that the phew was even getting into my hair. It was right hard on Uncle Shorty's arms when I rode the cultivator, though, since that meant that he had to be carrying my weight all the time so the plows did not dig too deep. But he did not care. He liked me, and I knew that. A little fat boy never had it so good. The river was on my right, the railroad on my left, and all the while I was standing neck-deep in a field of corn. There was a little grove of walnut trees up on the bank and a well pump and a big concrete water trough. With good shade and cold water, what could be better?

We would plow the corn rows out with the horse first. Then Fanny, the old horse, was taken up on the railroad right-of-way and turned loose to graze on the honeysuckle and weeds. I guess she liked those weeds. She never wandered off, just moved from one big clump of weeds and grass to another, eating her fill. I never saw much grass there, so it was good that she liked eating weeds too.

Then we would set to chopping weeds. When I was little, this field looked to be a mile long. Daddy and Shorty would take to telling me about the Old Flannigan Farm across the river. Daddy said that his first paying job was getting water for men working in the horseshoe in the cornfield on the Flannigan Farm.

"Working in the horseshoe" referred to how the river made a funny long U-shaped turn and the land around it lay in the shape of a horseshoe. In the morning, men would ride the ferry over from Whitethorne and walk to the main barns. Daddy said that since there were no water springs on this side of the horseshoe, water had to be carried in the wagon or gotten from the opposite side of the river. His job was to swim across the river to the Tommy Bottom with a one-gallon jar for spring water. Going over the jar was empty and served as a float; going back it was full and tended to slow you down. Pappy would make this trip three or four times a day. As he remembered it, if he got tired he would paddle the boat, but it was lots more fun to swim the river.

One of the jobs that sticks in my mind is hoeing corn. Daddy and many others tell this same story, so I think that it is accurate. Every man working corn put his dinner bucket on a small lunch wagon that was taken to end of the cornfield and left there. Each man hoed two rows of corn from the start of the field downriver to his lunch, ate and hoed two rows back. Often big boys did the hoeing, and grown men did the plowing of the row centers.

Another neat story of this era told of corn and wheat being ground into meal at the old mill on Tom's Creek. The old mill still stands today at the mouth of the creek on New River and is on the Historical Register.   In the early 1900s spring, summer and fall, small quantities of grain were carried over to the mill on the ferryboat.

During the winter, in the early part of the century, the river still froze hard. Grain was carried over the ice on New River with horse-drawn wagons. Uncle Lake once told me that wagons would cut a groove in the ice, but it did not break. The next trip they would just move over to an unscratched place. He also told me that he and my Great Uncle Delmer would ice skate from the boat landing at the White Rock near Grandmother's house all the way to the Grist Mill. For fun, sometimes they would even race the trains down the mountain. With a big smile and a faraway look in his eyes, he recalled, "We just never won."

They just never won. It always sounded like a title of one of the pictures on the Currier and Ives calendar in

Grandmother's room. Uncle Lake's eyes said it was a long time ago when life just seemed to be much simpler. For a second he was almost dreaming.

The story I would ask for over an over was the one about the big coal rock. I was setting by the concrete water tank under the big walnut's shade. They started with, "Right where we are setting now, there used to be a large two-story house. Jimmy Snider and his family once lived here in this house. It burned down about the time of the 1920 flood. Always keep in mind that, "when that old slow New River wants to, it can come very fast and wash away houses and animals and destroy everything in its path."

Living along the river, you know that danger can come from anywhere. Sometimes in the past alot of people would steal coal off the trains for the winter. To steal coal, what you did was get on the coal cars near Whitethorne and ride them up toward the Snider houses. When you got near the houses, you started pitching off lumps of coal. Later you came back with a horse and the big four-wheel wagon to pick up the coal for winter. Everyone up and down the railroad did this. All of my uncles stole coal too. They said that they took many a sled and two-horse wagon full of coal up the hill to Mammaw's house.

This particular time, Jimmy Snider found a rather large lump of coal and managed to push it over to the side of the coal car. The lump was very large, and he did not want to have to bust it up to drag it out on a horse-drawn sled, so he decided to push it off the coal car near his house. As the train got closer to the house, he gave this big lump a push. Down off the railroad right of way it went, right into his yard. It kept going, though, and ran right through the front door into the house, taking the doorjamb with it. In one version, the coal lump even broke the door facing and knocked the leg off of the eating table. If you are of a mind, I will leave it to you to fix this door and reattach the table leg.

Dogs: Maxine, Spike, Pappy, Old Jim Dog, Arthur

Dogs were an important part of growing up on River Ridge. I guess that is true everywhere. About the first dog I can remember was old Maxine. She was about half collie, half border collie and half coyote maybe. Her hair was long black, white and brown, and stuck out in every direction. Her roving eyes were dark brown, and she belonged to no one. Maxine just came and went whenever she wanted, and everyone on the hill fed her. I think she had a good life. She kind of slept where she was.

One time we were plowing the potato patch below the pond, and on the way home Daddy grabbed a-holt of old Fanny's tail for a little help up the steep part of the hill. (Fanny was our draft horse.) Like Daddy, I grabbed a-holt of Maxine's tail for a little help up the hill. She just put her paws in four-wheel drive and kept on going. I can remember watching her walk our milk cows to the barn in the evenings. Sometimes she did the same for Mr. Luther Snider, who lived across the road from us. She was slow coming to the barn unless one of the cows did not want to come. She then got a little rough so she could show the cow who the real boss was.

When we were little, if she caught the fleas, we did too. Once in awhile, after I had been bathed in the last of the laundry water, Grandmother would pick up Maxine and give her a bath, holding her so there was nothing sticking out of the water but her head. "Those fleas that ain't drowned will run to the top of her head, and I will kill them with lye soap," was Grandmother's explanation. No, I never did see Maxine get any soap in her eyes. We all laughed as we watched her try to swim around in that tub with Grandmother just hanging on.

I can remember sleeping and playing in the barn loft in Maxine's dog bed when I was a very little boy. When she had puppies, we would pet them, make over them, talk baby talk to them and scratch their small bellies all day long. Every milking, Shorty would put out fresh milk for them in the morning and at night. "Puppies like fresh milk," Uncle Short would laugh and say. He'd set there with me and make sure that each puppy got a drink. "Them damn big ones will lick up all the milk if you ain't careful, and the runt won't get any."

My mother spoke of a distant relative coming up to the house; I will call him Great Uncle Cledious. Since at the time of this story, I must not have been more than four or five years old, I must rely on my mother's recounting.

211

Uncle Cledoius very rarely ever came, but he still came far too often for my liking. He was a very loud and boastful person, who was always spitting tobacco juice in the coal scuttle. I was glad that the newer coal scuttle, the one with no holes in it, was setting by the stove. The big gobs of tobacco spit would hiss and sputter when new coal was dumped in the coal stove. I don't think many on my side of the family liked him much.

According to Mother, the reason Great Uncle Cledious came this particular time was to jump on Uncle Shorty, "By damn, I have heard that you have gave away one of them damn puppies. By damn, you ort to be selling them pups. They are worth something; that bitch will work cattle. Them pups can be taught to work cattle and sheep, too. Hell boy, you ain't going to ever have a pot to pee in or a window to pitch it out of if you don't start looking after your pennies!"

I think this relative was right in some ways. I just never learned to watch my pennies very well either, and I truly don't have much of anything today but fun, happiness and a great life. Just maybe, money ain't all there is in this life.

Later when my butt was higher off the ground, I can remember Pride Arrington had one of Maxine's pups that rode in his old red International truck with him. I do not think that this dog ever worked anything but his jaws while eating and sometimes barking. Pride liked to feed him some of whatever he was eating. "Someday he will be worth something," Mr. Pride would laugh and say. All the while, the dog ate another bag of potato chips. If I ever got in the truck with that dog, I had to have all of my snacks already eaten. He would give out kind of a low growl and then eat my food.

In my life on River Ridge a whole host of dogs came and went. We had beagles — some for hunting and some for selling puppies from. One of the funniest dogs there ever were was "Old Pappy." He had short ears and short legs, but he left four tracks and one narrow path in the snow. He did not like to come out of the barn when there was much snow on the ground for obvious reasons. I reckon he didn't cotton to draggin' his tallywhacker through the snow.

Yes, Old Pappy. If dogs could have voted, he would have worn a Grover Cleveland Button. Mason Graham, the county dog warden, brought him to the house and said: "Now boys, he will hunt. I have had him for a long time, and he is eating me out of a dog pound. I think you all ort to have him."

The more Mason talked, the louder he spoke. At age 16, I could hear someone pulling my leg. Mason was shooting a line of bull crap. No dog that good was coming from the dog pound! The more I listened, I started thinking possibly he even pointed birds and carried a variety of shotgun shells, too. Daddy, Uncle Shorty and me just listened and were taken in by the yarn.

That was all it took. Everyone on the hill wanted him. We pinned him up in the barn loft for a couple of weeks and fed him the best table scraps on the hill. This was to make him get accustomed to the place and us kids. Within a few minutes,

Pappy was already comfortable with the new place, and it was real obviously he wasn't going anywhere. In a few weeks he went from fit and trim to fatter than a town dog! You had to wake him up to feed him. Old Pappy was old and gray around his mouth and eyes. He was clearly old enough to vote, and he did not like being out in the sunlight. He much preferred spending his days eating scraps and sleeping.

One day when we turned him loose, he just came to life like he had been shot out of a cannon. He took to the hill above the potato patch and marched right under the blackberry briars. Out of nowhere he seemed to be able to find a rabbit. A rabbit could not shake him off of the trail. As fat and old as he was, he could flat out run the long-eared fellers.

"Have you seen anything like that?" everyone laughed. "He seems like he is making a rabbit right out of thin air. He is the real deal." That afternoon it was like everybody wanted to take Old Pappy home with them. He was like an honored guest, held in as high esteem as the dog warden.

Day after day we walked him out over the hill, and day after day the short-legged dog went under the thick briar patch and marched through the tall stickweeds and did battle with the sticker bushes and brought out a rabbit. It looked like Old Pappy was the "find" of a lifetime.

Well, everything went well until the opening day of rabbit season. No one had been more excited to see the first day of rabbit season than the Lytton Men on the hill. Them old single-barrel 12-gauges were cleaned and well-oiled, because they had not seen action in six months or more and were expected to work hard this day! All of the women on the hill had started to grease up the cast iron Dutch ovens in anticipation of the opening day of rabbit season. Everyone could just taste the first bite of fried rabbit and that thick, milky-white rabbit gravy and hot buttered biscuits. (Second only in taste to squirrel gravy.) "We eat like town people tonight," said Daddy. "You just wait and see."

We were all just petting Old Pappy on the head, scratching him on the back, and leading him down to the railroad right-of-way. There he was turned loose and off he went. Like in the past, he jumped a rabbit and turned that thing right toward us. "BOOM" the 12-gauge roared to life. Before the sound died away, even before the dead rabbit could be picked up, "Old Pappy" was nowhere to be seen. It was like he vanished right into thin air.

Everyone said that they had missed the rabbit and shot him. We looked for him, but he was gone. The remainder of the day was spent beating the brush, tramping though the high weeds, wading through briar patches in an effort to jump a rabbit. Old Pappy had just vanished for sure.

Later that day, we learned that Old Pappy had gone home to the barn. I have never seen such a gun-shy dog. When we found him, he was shaking like he was trying to crap out a peach seed, a very large peach seed. He spent the last days of his life setting on the porch with Jim Dog. A car backfiring would send him to the barn loft. Somewhere in his past I think people were mean to Old Pappy, but he did live out the last days of his life in comfort with lots of gravy, squirrel gravy that is. Little rabbit gravy was found on River Ridge.

There were others, too, like Pepper, Arthur, Alice, Jim, Qieque, Original Spike, New Spike, and more. Original Spike was a big boxer who lived on the dog chain at Uncle Nelson's. About all of us kids were scared to death of him. If he got loose, he came looking for us kids, not to bite, but to chase after us. Sometimes I think that he liked my brother, Michael, the most. One time he knocked Michael down and stood over him while he ate his peanut butter sandwich. He and Mike had an ongoing peanut butter sandwich battle. But in the end, Michael fooled him. Mike made a peanut butter sandwich with a jar of peanut butter on the slice of bread. This was back in the day when peanut butter was about as thick as window calk and as sticky as plumbers' putty. Sometimes Mother would have to mix butter or honey into the peanut butter to get it out of the jar.

Mike was ready when Spike came after him. Spike ate the peanut butter sandwich in one big bite and almost choked to death before he staggered to the pond for drink of water. "Take that," we all yelled when he took to rolling and coughing and scratching at his face with both paws.

Spike wasn't always full of peanut butter and fun, though. He was a world-class groundhog killer. When he went on the hunt, he always brought back his trophy. Every bone in its body would be broken. He would lay the dead ground hog at the back door for you to see and admire. The problem was, some of his trophies might have been dead for a few days when he brought them in. Mother would scream: "Somebody needs to come get that damn stinkin' groundhog and bury it quick, or there will be no breakfast here today. Open the windows and doors, and let some fresh air in." The same screams were heard down at Grandmother's and Aunt Tootie's, too.

One morning we were all lined up waiting for the school bus. All of us kids and Old Spike, too. He liked the school bus and would have gone to school if we had let him ride it. All of a sudden, another dog appeared across the road in Mr. Luther's field. Spike took to growling and barking. He stepped into the road to make his point, and a fast car hit him. He went up in the air at least ten feet and flew through the air like Superman or Underdog. He hit the ground, rolled over a few times and then took off running like he had been shot out of a cannon.

For a long time there on Guinea Mountain, I had no dogs. For some reason, people found my house a good place to drop off their troubled dogs. I think they knew I had a soft heart and would keep the dogs and feed them. Over just a few months, I went from no dogs to three.

One was a border collie named "Raisin Bran." He was one of the best car-chasing dogs I ever saw. Otis, my neighbor, commented, "Wonder what he thinks he's going to do with that car if he catches up with it?" Odis and I would set up on the road bank and drink gallons of sweet tea and marvel at how fast he was. Raisin Bran never missed a car; he could run all day. The dust did not seem to bother him a bit. "He ort to catch black lung or something, breathing in all that road dust. I am starting to catch it myself setting here watching him," said Otis. Then we would just laugh and watch him go.

Raisin Bran almost never barked. If a person came to the house he did not know, he'd just nipped at their heels every time they walked past him. Me, I always made sure where he was before I left the house. I guess I never did get to know him. Chuck Shorter came over in the spring to shear New Spike, but he did not shear Raisin Bran. Chuck thought he was too inclined to bite and could "just stay hot all summer."

Quee was an almost-grown Rottweiler when she was dropped at our front door. She was covered with mange so bad that the veterinarian said that putting her to sleep was a humane option. But, Miss Dianna, the little six-year-old girl wholived with us just started to cry.

Instead the veterinarian gave me dog mange shampoo. At the time Quee had almost no hair, but the scratches, sores and marks made her look like Queequeg, the tattooed man in the book Moby Dick. That's how she got her name. After several thousand treatments over a few months, she took to growing new hair again. She started eating regularly, too, and she turned into one big dog. If she was in the house, a visitor or me had better knock and let her know who was at the door. Quee became real protective of her feed bowl and those that fed her. She and Miss Dianna slept together. She was a lot like

Raisin Bran when it came to biting: she liked it. But she liked to do her biting inside the house. Outside she was gentle as a lamb and would set with me and Otis and watch Raisin Bran chase cars, but never join in.

Then there was "Spike the Vicious," who was big, but was so lazy he would set down to eat and drink. One very cold time on Guinea Mountain, my neighbor that lived on the next ridge called me: "Are you missing one real big yellow dog?"

"Well, there is one that sometimes hangs around here but he ain't my dog. I have not seen hide nor hair of him in awhile," I answer.

"Your big yellow dog is over here in the house, and won't come out. Every time we try to put him outside, he growls at us. You need to come get this beast. If he goes to the bathroom. it will be a bucket full."

Well I went over to get the thing, and I guess that is the day we started to own him. When a car pulled in, Spike would bark, Raisin Bran would start trying to bite the tires and Quee was just big enough to hold your attention.

One time, the folks from the local church came over to ask me to join their congregation. They came over just once, I am sorry to say. They got out of their car at normal speed with their Sunday-best clothes on, but then ran straight into the house like the devil himself was after them. There was no knocking on the door, and they were cussing at me like sailors: "Holy shit, you have got to do something about them damn mean-assed dogs!" One of them must have had a sausage biscuit in her pocket. I don't think they were used to having dogs get after them much. Miss Dianna just started to pet the dogs, and they rolled over and licked her while the church ladies made a break for the door.

Unfortunately, there had been a shooting in another county. The shooters had run downriver and were holed up not far from my house on Guinea Mountain. All of sudden, the Giles County High Sherriff was standing in the house. Again, there was no knocking on the door. The big Rottweiler was standing close and peering at up him with a sour look on her face. I go running into the kitchen, and the sheriff screams at me "What kind of animals do you keep up here?"

"Did they bite you?"

"No. Hell no, I was running too fast. But I could hear their teeth chomping! I came up here to warn you about all the commotion down over the hill. Now I want to warn you that if them dogs kill my prisoner I am going to be real mad. How in the world do you propose I get back to my car?"

The dogs never really bit anyone; but you could put down a five-dollar bill in the yard, and no one was going to pick it up. About everyone knew about them. If someone came to visit, they always blew the car horn and asked me to "hold them dogs." The second visit, the dogs were in the car looking for food and wanting to be petted on the head.

One time, in a very weak moment, for some unknown

reason I decided I needed a basement. Digging the basement under the new addition on the house was a bigger job than I had planned on. I had to hire some boys to help me. They told me they needed extra money for the prom, and rather than work a few evenings earlier in the week they wanted to work the morning of the prom. We started around 3:30 a.m. on Saturday morning and stopped at 4:00 p.m. They wanted an early start, so they could get off early.

I am setting at the kitchen table drinking coffee when their pickup truck drives up and stops. I hear both truck doors open and one close quickly. The motion lights on the porch come on, and the yard is filled with screaming. I go running out the door and find one boy pinned in the cab of his truck and one setting on the top of the truck. All three dogs are just walking around the truck looking up and barking. These guys are treed for sure! I hold the dogs, and the boys make a break for the house. Willy said, "Mr. Lytton, it was dark, and the dogs could not see who to bite first. So the small one ran up on the porch and cut the light on, and then all three just charged."

"Do they bite?" they asked.

"Have they ever bit you?" I answer.

"No, but I think they wanted too!" came two answers.

Both boys worked real hard, and when they went to leave I paid them off in cash money for the prom. They had big dinner plans and wanted to impress the girls. The only problem was they fell asleep at the dance, and both girls left the dance with different people. The cleanup crew had to waken them after the dance so they, too, could go home. The moral of the story: don't dig dirt from way before daylight until 4:00 p.m. just before your prom. You just might fall dead asleep with your pockets full of green money and miss a most wonderful evening!

Making and Walking on Stilts

Early on in my life, the smallest of things would entertain me for hours. For example, we were down in May's Holler, where Uncle Shorty and Daddy were cutting fence posts. I think that I was just in the way. I was too small to work real hard, and they were too busy to keep an eye out for dangers. They had to come up with something to both entertain me and keep me busy. Most important, they needed to get me out of the way.

To accomplish this, they made me a set of stilts by cutting small limbs off of a locust tree with small lateral branches that were no more than 10 to 12 inches off the ground. They just handed them to me and said, "Now, go up to the potato patch and play with these stilts."

When I said I didn't know what to do with them, Daddy took the stilts and positioned them in front of him. He stepped on, clumsily took a short step and almost fell off. Uncle Shorty started to laugh and insisted, "Give me the damn things." Then he took a very shaky short step or two. He was no better at walking on stilts than Daddy.

Over the course of the next two hours, I never even got a chance to try. They just kept on until they got back to their youthful proficiency. Me, I just watched and laughed. When I got my turn, I just could not balance on them at all. Both men walked by my side for a while. Before you know it I was taking a clumsy step or two. They then laughed at me. "Oh hell, you got it. Walk to Price's Fork a time or two, and you will be among the best."

A short time later, Uncle Shorty wanted me help him. So he and I walk to the barn, drag out two two-by-fours and lay them on the hog-scalding platform. "I think it is about time I teach you to build things," he said. He then showed me where to hold blocks of wood, and I nailed when I was told to. Before you know it, we had made me a brand new set of "Walking Stilts." Uncle Shorty promised, "Them won't hurt your feet like them locust limbs." I walked on them for weeks, and after that kind of lost interest.

Some four or five years later, I took up muskrat-trapping for a living. Heck, I put myself through the winter of 1964 muskrat-trapping. I had traps set on both sides of Tom's Creek. All went well before the creek froze. I would wade from one side of the creek to the other. Yes, it was cold, but I had a lot of ground to cover and wasn't too much worried about being cold. I never got wet much past my knees. One time I tried to walk across the thin ice and fell in. By the time I got out I was wet from head to foot, and I ran home as fast my fat little legs could carry me. Mom and Daddy did not say much other than:

"A person could freeze to death if he got trapped under an ice sheet. Just leave them traps on the far side of the creek until it gets warm. You can go get them then."

Well, I tried to pay attention, but the chance of catching a muskrat on the far bank was weighing heavy on me. Before the creek froze over solid again, I found me two two-by-fours and made myself a set of stilts like the ones Uncle Shorty had shown me years earlier. The foot pegs were three feet off the ground. I found an open riffle just above Jonny Stepson's house, and I just walked back in forth on these new stilts. I never had one problem. I think it was because of the quality of the training I had when I was watching Shorty and Daddy cutting post.

I just loved to do things with Daddy and Shorty. I learned that they were not always old men. They had a great sense of humor. When I was a child, I truly thought that Uncle Shorty and Daddy both owned me. In many ways they did. One of these days I am going to make a set of stilts for my little grandbaby girls. They, too, may want to go to the creek.

Things You Don't See Anymore and That Is Good

I find it so funny how my mind works. Just a few days ago, I walked into an antique shop. I do this all the time. As I wandered around, I saw chairs, tools and old blue canning jars. There were few things that I did not know well from my own youth. I even saw the faces of men and women who had been dead for years. Yet, there they were in my mind just canning away or building things with the old tools.

All of a sudden, I was taken by a small glass box labeled "musical bones." My mind had been wandering before, but now I was focused on remembering. As I looked at the box of finely carved bones, I could see Roosevelt Washington Franklin cutting the core out of an apple with a leg bone from a lamb and handing me a slice. The bone was boiled clean, free of marrow and carefully shaped like a long spoon with a sharp edge. It still had the knee joint attached to be used as the handle when it pushed through the apple. "Made it myself. Old people just know how to do things," said Mr. Roosevelt. "Old bones can be used for lots of things."

He had made a flute or whistle out of the leg bone of a turkey. Turkey bones are very hard and break easy. The most intriguing bone tool of all was a bone marrow remover. It was made on the same order as the apple corer, but from the wing bone of a turkey. A long and thin tool, it could reach far back into a small bone.

I asked Daddy and Shorty if people eat bone marrow, pretty sure I wouldn't like it. "I think the main reason Roosevelt showed you them things was to make you ask these questions," said Uncle Shorty. "He's kind of laughing at us right now."

"People eat bone marrow all the time and never think about it," they both answered. "Have you ever seen Mamaw and your mother put bones into soup and brown beans to add flavor? Some of that flavor comes from meat still hanging on the bone. Maybe the bone has flavor, too, but for sure some flavor comes from the bone marrow."

"Well, my soup- and bean-eating days are over!" I said.

I had never seen tools like these or ever wanted to. I think old people had no television to watch, and when they ran out of wood to chop, or when the potatoes had been laid by, they must have set around and dreamed up new stuff to do. Making an apple core remover and a bone marrow remover from bones must have either taken a lot of dreaming up or a lot of boredom. Either way, they were just eerie somehow.

Did I Really See What I Saw?

It was in the fall of 1975. I was working for the Virginia Tech agriculture farms. This day I was on the farm in Catawba, VA, which is not far from both Salem and Blacksburg. I was disking a large field not too far from what used to be the Catawba Tuberoses Sanitarium. At this point, the facility was being operated for senior living.

The corn had been chopped out of this field about two weeks earlier, and now it was time to plant a cover crop. I was using an old David Brown Tractor to pull a 14' disk across the field. The early fall season was on us. The sky was still as blue as indigo, and there was almost no air stirring. The sun brought out a sweat on my back, but the motion of the air created by the David Brown quickly dried the front of me, leaving a very pleasant chill. There was the fresh smell of leaves drifting in from the mountain as they just were starting to fall. I could pick out all the maple trees on the side of the mountain by their light orange, yellow and red color. Color was starting to show on the other trees, too. But the big oaks were still green.

Add the very pleasant smell of the woods, the tanginess of just-cut grass from up around the old hospital, the loamy contribution from freshly turned earth and spice it with the sharp blasts from the tractor's diesel exhaust. Yes, it was something great! The old David Brown eased itself down each small hill and grunted out dark black smoke as it strained its way back up the other side.

As I rounded the corner, I saw a hearse coming up the hard-top road headed for the old hospital. I hate to say it, but this was not an uncommon sight. Well, I just kept working up the earth, making ready to plant a cover crop of rye. After an hour, possibly two, I saw the hearse make its way back down the road, and as it passed me I stopped the David Brown, stood up and took off my hat. Why I did this I do not know; I never had before.

Just about the time I was making ready to set down and start the tractor, a small kind of dust devil blew up right out of nowhere and stopped right in from of me. For an instant, there stood the ghost of the old man in that hearse. He said: "Now, just don't be worried about me. Life has been good. Why, I have run very fast, tasted about everything there ever was and experienced about everything this old body would allow. You had best do the same. Make sure to remember how great your life has been when you get old. Sometimes when you are old, the memories are all you have." As the long black car pulled away, the old man spoke in a very youthful voice. "I see you son, but right now I got other things I got to go do."

I never saw him again. Oh, to be quite honest, maybe I did not see him at all. Possibly I just wanted to. He was my first and only ghost, and he seemed right nice. Truth be told, I never gave him one moment's thought until I started writing this collection of stories. I realized that. . .well, I guess I have run fast and far. I have eaten up some great stuff and drunk some fine wines and white licker, too. I have done about all this old body could ever want. Read on and you will see what I mean. And I must say, I thank that old ghost for his encouragement.

A Story About Moonshine

Thunder Road weren't no movie or book; it was a true real life story of the Appalachian Mountain and her people!

I think this short little story about moonshine in a way sums up the true Appalachian interest in that fine liquid. Through the years I have heard this story told two or three different times and in different ways. This is my version. I have taken the liberty of adding in Uncle Fred Lytton's, too, you know, just to make it more interesting and readable.

Me and Uncle Fred are setting on the river bank down by the White Rock. We have been there for more than a four hours and have not gotten a bite of anything. As the hours passed the level of moonshine in the ½ gallon Mason jar has steadily gone down. During that same time, the number of minnows in the bucket has gone down as well. There is one right scrawny little minnow left. We have been avoiding him all day, because he is so little and puny. It is now or never for the little scrawny minnow. "I don't even know why we kept him," I said.

Uncle Fred looks at me with a funny look on his face. Saving the best for last. He reaches down in the bucket and grabs up the scrawny little minnow. Then he takes a slow pull from the shine jar, and it truly does seem to wake him up and give him more energy. So Uncle Fred drops the scrawny little minnow down in the moonshine jar and lets him swim around a minute or two.

When I ask when he is going to take the minnow out, he says: "Just a minute or two more. He will let you know when he has had enough. He needs to get relaxed and tufted up a little in his own way."

All of a sudden that minnow takes to jumping and almost jumps out of the jar. "Well that ort to be enough," says Uncle Fred, as he reaches into the jar, catches up that minnow and hooks him onto the line. He then casts that minnow about halfway across the river.

It wasn't more than two minutes before Fred's line took to jumping, and the pole bent double. Uncle Fred and little minnow had hooked a big one. It took more than ten minutes for Uncle Fred to get the big catfish up on the bank. I was shocked to see that the minnow had grabbed that big catfish right behind the head and was holding on.

Uncle Fred put the minnow back in the moonshine for another minute, and then cast him down deep into the White Rock Hole. The two of them went on to catch enough catfish for supper at my house and Grandmother's, before Uncle Fred turned that little minnow loose. You can take from that story what you wish. But there's nothing that a little clean licker won't improve.

As I write this essay, I think the popularity of moonshine is growing. Hardly a week goes by that a person doesn't call me or stop me on the sidewalk and ask, "Where can I get a jar of moonshine?" If they ask for a jar I know that they know what they are talking about; those that ask for a bottle — well, I just keep walking. They are shocked when I say, "I haven't a clue."

I think there is a resurgence in the nostalgia of moonshine. People just want to be a part of the experience and do not truly understand moonshine and XXX on a bottle. Today, I still run across people who want me to have a drink of their shine. Some are taken aback when I am reluctant to take a taste. I am a firm believer that good shine is hard to find, and if I don't know where it came from I do not want a drink! But I love their stories.

There have been many stories and tall tales told about moonshine in Appalachia. I am still shocked to learn who once made shine. If half of the local stories are true, there were once many stills scattered across my local Appalachian mountain. More shocking are the names associated with these operations. For example, my daddy said when I was a 10-year-old we went to the mill every other Saturday to have feed ground, and he "always came home with one sack that he was very careful with." A half or a gallon of shine would be in the sack.

One of the funniest stories was about a man who ran a cleaning service. He came to homes in the early 1960s and picked up everything from dirty baby diapers to clothes that needed to be dry-cleaned. If you wanted moonshine, you put in your order, and it would be delivered when your clean clothes were returned.

There are too many stories to recount. Some, if true, just might get a person in trouble even today with their families. I doubt the law would have much interest after all these years. I never saw these things when I was growing up, but I have no reason to stop believing these stories.

Moonshine was a business and run like a business. There was and still is a code of silence associated with past and present moonshine production. There were those who made shine, those who sold it and those who transported the illegal alcohol. Often there was a third party involved, and those were the marketing people. What I think is most interesting is that many times none of the parties knew much about each other. "If you did not know where you got the shine, you could not testify in court as to where it came from." There was and still is a safety in ignorance.

I think that during my upbringing many local men drank and liked moonshine more than they did whiskey and liquors bought from the ABC Store in Christiansburg. Words my father and my uncles used became almost part of my early vocabulary. For example,

"Yes, she's good stuff. Did you see that blue flame?"

"Damn, look how it beads up real nice? Look at how it rolls over that jar. That has got to be some of the best clear liquor I ever saw."

234

"Why, that don't have much of bad taste going down, now does it?"

"This here must be running upwards of 90 to 100 proof, or I will eat your hat. If it is that hot, you might need that hat of yours for a chaser." (90 proof is about 45 percent alcohol.)

"Don't that liquor leave a fine taste in your mouth and about the right amount of burn?"

Today, like in days gone by, much of the moonshine is proofed with clear spring water, and brought down to about 80 proof or 40% alcohol, much like alcohol purchased at the ABC Store. As a teenager and young adult, I liked the hot, throat-burning, higher percentage alcohol. The burn was like a fire, and I could just feel manhood coming over me. Today, I know just how foolish I was. I like the lower proof moonshine, and good 80 proof is just fine. Lower proof Apple Pie is just fine too. "A ladies' drink," my mentors called it. At my age it is strong enough, but I still like a throat-warming burn.

Today, I can be giving a talk about growing up in Appalachia and my dad's and uncles' love of moonshine, when out of nowhere women and men will start telling me of their own experiences. Often all I have to say is "This sure does bead up real nice," and a whole new set of stories starts.

Another thing I have observed is that women must have liked shine as much as the men. This is based on their stories. Women seemed to like the lower-proof stuff, but sure drank their share. Now my mother and grandmother would not agree with this observation, because they did not like moonshine or any hard liquor.

In our house, there was always a pint Mason jar of moonshine in the medicine cabinet. Daddy filled a jar with hard rock candy peppermint sticks and moonshine. When I had the croup or a cough, I was given two or three real big spoonsful. "That stuff will make the hair grow on you in the important parts and put you right to sleep!" Elmer would say. "Hell, I just even might get to sleep tonight, too."

As I said earlier, there was and still is a quiet, unspoken secret code of silence that goes along with moonshine. If you knew who was running a still, no word was ever spoken in reference to whom, when or where. If a person in the community had a fast car and was hauling moonshine, again no one spoke about it out in public. Everyone in the whole community was in on the secret, but no outsider was ever told or had a clue. If you informed the sheriff or "the law," you were shunned and all but banished by the good folks of the community. The still was kept in a most secret place, and few ever knew it was there. You could squirrel hunt within a few yards and never know it was there. When the still was running, you would never be allowed to get near the location. Someone would tell you to "get your butt out of here and don't come back either." You knew the meaning, and you left and did not come back neither.

Here is what I mean. Recently, I met Miss Eveloine Muncy. She was a most respected retired schoolteacher from a county in another region of this fine state. She said she has taught school about as long as she can remember. Like me, she is trying to learn how to be retired. Not too long ago, I was part of this workshop for retired teachers. During the first break after my presentation, she came and sat down right next to me, chuckled and said, "This here punch we are drinking needs a little life to it, don't it?" Well, there was a time when I would have agreed. What do I mean? I keep a jar on the shelf all the time, never know just when someone will mix up one of these punch concoctions and it might need a little spark. She winked and got up, then just stepped away.

Miss Eveloine said that when she was a little girl she often helped out around the still: "It wasn't work for a little girl, but Daddy needed help and there weren't any boys, so I did it. Sometimes my job was nothing more than setting off a distance on the rise and watching the valley below. If I saw somebody, I had a 410 shotgun with me, and I would shoot up in the air. Sometimes I would put rings and lids on quart and half-gallon jars. We did not have any of the plastic milk jugs. Break a glass jar, and your ass might get broke."

She also watched the look on people's faces when they came to her house looking for shine. "Often they never said a word. You just knew by the look on their face what they wanted. Daddy took their money and took to walking though the field, and in a few minutes you would hear their truck drive off. I was never to touch the money or join him on one of his nightly walks," said Miss Eveloine Muncy. "That was grown man's work. White licker paid for me to go to Longwood College.

"I got to ride with Daddy almost every time he made a delivery. Police would not pull a car over with a father and little girl in the car. I was his 9- year insurance policy," she continued. "Daddy was not a big-time moonshiner. He never had more than 10 or 12 half gallons in the car. Back in the forties and early fifties that wasn't enough to fool with. Another thing was, Daddy always delivered the moonshine to a Methodist Church in town. While we were at the church meeting singing and praying, the shine was removed from the car and money was put up under the floor mat."

I met an older fellow who told me that his grandfather was a moonshiner. By day he was employed helping build the Blue Ridge Parkway. He drove an old dump truck. By night he worked the family still. He transported licker in the company dump truck. During breaks he would sell pints and half pints of moonshine to the workers building the Parkway. The old fellow telling me this story said that as a child his job was to walk the ditches along the public road and pick up old liquor bottles with caps that had been pitched out the car windows. The bottles were washed and re-filled with moonshine for his granddad to carry to work.

One person told me that his family ran a small store in town. They sold about the same things as all small stores — canned goods, tobacco, cigarettes and a little gasoline. One big difference was they had a popcorn machine. There was always moonshine hidden under the cooling popcorn. If you wanted moonshine, it was sold to you in small bottles or jars hidden in bags of cold popcorn. Even some of the local police bought a bag of popcorn from his daddy. If the popcorn was fresh and hot, you would have to go somewhere else for your shine.

Today, I must admit, if there is a bottle of shine around, I want to smell and taste a small amount of it. I have heard some people say that moonshine is a tasteless form of alcohol. All I can respond is, "We never drank from the same Mason jar." To me, moonshine has almost no taste when you put it in your mouth. The true taste comes as soon as you swish it around and swallow it down, when the life-giving liquid springs to life. I get a hot mealy-metallic flavor in the back of my mouth. This is followed by a true feeling that I have just swallowed a lit firecracker or maybe a stick of burning kindling wood. If you have taken a real big gulp, you might think that your throat is bleeding, but it truly ain't. That warm glow goes all the way down to my navel and just kind of stays there for a while.

How do you make moonshine? The ingredients are right simple and can be found at your grocery store. Cracked corn, oatmeal, sugar, yeast and water are about all that is needed. First, dump the corn and oatmeal into a large pot and add in the water. Add in the yeast. Let the mixture set for a few days until it starts to ferment. Just like when making yeast bread, the yeast will start to grow within a few hours. Once the yeast has finished breaking down the starch into sugar, the mash is ready to run or be cooked in the "pot still." The mash is dumped into the still and cooked on low heat. Run the temperature up to about 150° to 160°. You do not want the mixture to reach the water boiling temperature. All the steam is collected in a copper cap attached to copper coil. This is the worm, a coil of copper tubing is kept in a tank or barrel of cold water used to convert the steam into liquid. The clear liquid that drips from the copper pipe is alcohol.

The very first alcohol to come out is collected and not used. Also, the very last of the run is not used. The moonshiner wants the middle of the run. This is the good stuff. At this time, the moonshine may possibly be 160 proof or 80% pure alcohol. The alcohol is collected and dumped back into the still and cooked a second and sometimes a third time. The more time the alcohol is distilled, the higher the quality. One X on the old jars meant one time through the still. Two XX meant two times through the still. Three XXX meant three times through the still.

Each time the moonshine is distilled, more impurities are removed and the smoother and more clear the liquid becomes. Some people just might be tough enough to drink X, but not me. XX, I can do, but I like the XXX kind.

It takes an experienced person to proof licker correctly and the same way each time. It is not a good marketing plan to have customers liking shine that tastes one way this time a different way the next time. Both the moonshiner and drinker commonly shake a jar before it is sold. If right big bubbles form around the edge and vanish quickly, the moonshine is about 90 proof or 45% alcohol. Weaker, but still strong enough to set the hair on you!

There is a very young and nice, well-educated lady

that I have had the privilege of working with. One day we were taking her class on a field trip. It was a cool day, and, to make matters worse, she had a bad head cold. Between the coughing, sneezing and spitting, she informed me that if she lived to make it back home that afternoon she would go over to her daddy's house and get herself a few long drinks of shine. "Now that is the only way I know to clear this head out. Take a drink or two and swish it around in your mouth, and when you swallow air will go back into your sinuses in places that haven't had air in there for weeks."

What she was saying was kind of like what Milford Sherman said about moonshine: "Now hot licker will make your eyes water and the snot roll out of your head."

Not too long ago I was told a story about a lady who made licker not too far from where I was born. When her husband did not come home from World War II, she found herself in a situation where she just did not earn enough money to support her small family. She was working at the hardware store in town and needed more money, so she went to making moonshine. During the course of the story, I was told that the High Sheriff went to her hardware for a couple of screen-door hinges. While paying for them, he told the hardware lady that he needed to pin up his dogs for a night or two and let them rest some. There would be no coon hunting for them that night, he continued. He and the federal people had learned that shine was being made somewhere around town, and they were going to find that still.

Later in the week the federal people and the sheriff stopped by her house and enjoyed a glass of good cold spring water. "It is hot walking these mountains," they said. There was a big pot of green beans on the stove being canned and a large crock of cabbage being made into sauerkraut ready to carry to the cellar. The lady who told me this story said that the hardware lady was her mother and worked hard to keep a roof over their heads and beans in their bellies. Sometimes people have got to do what they have to do. "On our ridge top there was more money in selling liquor than raising corn."

I have met a lot of wonderful people as I have marched across the state marketing books. One of my most memorable encounters was at a store managed by a mother and daughter. One afternoon, I was putting *New River: bonnets, apple butter and moonshine* on the shelf of their store, when I was asked how I liked my moonshine.

"I like mine straight with a good cold jar of spring water for a chaser," I replied. "And you?"

"Well, it is coming on to summer, and we like a little flavor in our shine. No white licker for us. We like to chop up five or six ripe peaches and drop them down in a half-gallon of corn. After a day or two, we strain the liquor through a pair of old pantyhose and get all the peach pulp out. We keep it cold in the refrigerator. When we serve it, we just pour it over a water glass of ice cubes. Makes a good summertime drink," the pair explained. "We make peach, cherry and damson plum, too."

Another very interesting story I was told came from a man whose father was rumored to be a moonshiner. The High Sheriff shows up at this old man's house with a search warrant. The house, outbuildings and barns are searched, and nothing is found. "I still know you are makin licker," says the Sheriff.

"No sir, I have never made shine in my life," says the accused man.

"I think that I will arrest you anyway, and I am going to impound this barrel of hog feed, this rain barrel and this piece of copper tubing," says the High Sheriff.

To my knowledge, nothing was ever proven. But, some told me it was an effort to protect a known moonshiner. I think this might be true, because there seems like there is politics in about every part of life — even making moonshine. When I worked the mines with my uncles, I was always sent to the second man's house to purchase licker. Never to the first fellow's house in this story.

Uncle Shorty and a lot of men from River Ridge worked in the Conservation Corps or CCC Camp. This was a federal work program before World War ll. Uncle Shorty told me that about every payday, a car would stop by the Camp and a man would sell moonshine right out the trunk of his car in broad daylight. "If you had the money, he had the shine. Sometimes a little money got sent home to families."

Now That Is Something

"Now if that ain't stronger than a brick toilet," Elmer often remarked when he observed something strong or right tough. "Plus, you ain't moving that thing when they fill it up." (P.S. Elmer never said the word "toilet" in his whole life. I added "toilet" for the safety of your ears.)

I can just bet that this is something that you have never seen! When I was about eight or nine years old, I went to the hospital in Radford to have my tonsils removed. Back in 1960 a lot of people experienced this operation. I think it was done to help me with my sore throat and ear infections.

Well, as I was saying, I did have both tonsils removed. This operation did help me with the sore throat, but it did not help me with my upset stomach. No sir. The upset stomach came on when I would open the small mirrored door on the cabinet in Mom and Dad's bedroom. It slowly got better when I closed the small door. You see, when most people had their tonsils removed, the doctor pitched them over the hill for the dogs and cats to eat. Not my parents, no sir. They brought them swelled-up tonsils home with them in a small bottle of alcohol. Yes, you got it right. Daddy brought me home from the hospital in the old blue 1964 Suburban, and my tonsils in his shirt pocket!

I think they set in a cabinet until I was in high school. Then one day they were gone, but the memories of them remain until this very day.

Old Rock, Now There Was a Dog!

Sometimes you just got to be there to see the finer side of things. Or the meaning can get lost in translation.

When I was a child and even up into my young adulthood, stories of coon hunting filled the air around me. You just did not have to go anywhere special at all to hear a great, action-packed story. About ten years ago, a group of friends are going out to dinner. When we arrive at the restaurant, we learn no one has made a reservation, so we put our name on the lady's list and set down to wait for our turn to eat a big platter of fried fish.

As we wait, we start telling the old stories once again. I just love the old stories. Each time they are told new characters and new locations and never-before-mentioned exploits are added. Everyone knows the real story, but the new changes are most welcome and entertaining.

I like to change my friends' names in these stories. Never know when it might come home to haunt me. So I will tell you a fellow named Terry Albert passed this little story on to me.

Terry Albert is a masterful storyteller. When he tells a story, he becomes part of it. He can play all the characters, too. The best thing is he does not even know he is doing this. As the story starts, Terry kind of settles back and starts to talk real slow with numerous short pauses and uses many different voices for the characters. His mannerisms even change, too. It is like he is acting out the story, scene by scene.

It is has been very cold for more than a week, and everyone wants to get out for a little while, even Old Rock. (Old is not added to the name of a coon dog to indicate the dog's age, but to inform the reader of the years of experience — the pure knowledge and wisdom of hunt.) It is fair to say Old Rock has been around a tree a few times.

Come Saturday night Old Rock gets in the family car, finds a comfortable spot on the back seat and settles down for the long ride to the location selected for this night's hunt. As Old Rock dozes off, I can just bet he is dreaming of a shallow branch with fresh, muddy tracks leading through a small cornfield. The hot track heads up over a hill more than a mile away into a clump of big oaks.

On the way to Floyd County, which is more than 25 miles away, the men stop and pick up something to snack on and drink during the hunt. They come out of the store with a case of beer and set it on the seat by Old Rock. This wakes the dog up from a most wonderful hunting dream.

A cold Blue Ribbon apiece is opened, and the car's heater

is cranked up. They laugh and start telling each other stories about past hunting experiences. As they talk, Old Rock starts to moan and groan in a low voice. "I know you are getting ready Old Rock. We'll have you a coon real soon," says one of the men in a slightly drunk voice. The heater is still going full blast, too.

Another Blue Ribbon later, Old Rock starts to moan and groan again. "Just hang in there Old Rock. It ain't much farther now. In just a few more miles, I am going to get you one of the biggest coons you have ever seen," says the driver in a slightly more drunk voice.

In just a few more miles, Old Rock starts to kind of cough, kind of moan and kind of groan. There are other sounds, too. The driver says, "You had better check on Old Rock. If I did not know better, I be thinking he was back there a-pukin.

"Oh expletive, expletive. You need to pull the car over. Rock has done puked all over the case of Blue Ribbon beer."

The car is quickly stopped, and the beer is taken to the little branch and washed off. Rock gets a long-needed drink of water and a breath of cool air.

The beer is set on the back seat of the car, and Rock jumps in, too. Tranquility is restored. "Old Rock I am going to find you one of the biggest coons you have ever seen!"

You are now thinking: Did they ever find their way to mountain and find that big coon? Well, to be honest, I do not know, but everyone had a great time. Except maybe Old Rock.

Questions!

Now, if it smells like crap, well most likely that is what it is. All the smelling in the world ain't going to change it. That just is how the world is. My father, Elmer, sure had a way with words and a unique way of making a point.

People who have read my two earlier books sometimes call me and e-mail me with funny requests. I got a letter from lady asking me how to make fresh pork sausage. "We have raised a hog in the back lot and want to cure hams and make sausage. My question is simple: Just how do you go about making sausage anyway?"

One of the best questions was: "How do you fix a possum?" My answer was simple and quick. "I don't, and I ain't going to!"

"Well then, please give me a few suggestions on how eat a possum."

First off, you have got to catch a possum. Be real careful. They have a lot of teeth. The old timers would put a fresh-caught possum in a rabbit cage for a few weeks and feed it clean table scraps, lots of clean green grass and all the clean water the animal can drink. A little corn is good, too. Old timers say, "A possum is a very dirty eater. The rascal will eat about anything. So you need to cage that rascal for a while to clean it out."

My last suggestion was, "Please find Opossum in a cookbook that talks about nothing but cooking wild game, and follow the recipe to the letter! A greasy old possum is about as wild as any game there is."

Then I had one final comment: "Please don't ask me over for supper for a while."

Dressing Up

About every Sunday evening in summer, you could find Uncle Shorty dressed in his best clothes. That was his thin white shirt — one that you almost could see through — buttoned all the way to the collar and seersucker trousers. Through the spring and summer Uncle Shorty wore his blue and white seersucker pants. He had his hair parted in the middle and slicked back. Mother said when Shorty dressed up he was quite "a blade." I think that meant he looked sharp. Not to be outdone, my daddy, Elmer, had his seersucker suit, too.

When I was about six or seven years old, Jonas Salk discovered a polio vaccine. The vaccine was new, but the polio disease was not; there were two boys within one mile of my house who had polio. Our whole community arrived at the new Prices Fork School early one Saturday morning to be vaccinated. Both Daddy and Uncle Shorty got in line with the rest of us. People came in their Sunday best. Back then, people put on their good clothes to go out in public. People who normally wore bib overalls had on pants that needed a belt to keep them up.

Everyone looked at my family, especially Daddy and Uncle Shorty! Both were dressed to the tee. Clean, kind of crumply seersucker suits, shiny wingtip shoes, and small dress hats resting on the sides of their heads. They were sharp. Daddy was especially sharp when he stepped up and got his sugar cube with polio vaccine. He turned around and showed us how to put it in our mouths and eat it. "See, there ain't nothing to it," he said.

A few months ago, I went looking for a new sport coat. I found that I only tried on seersucker jackets. I tried on pink and white, but I did not like it. I found a whole suit of a light gray and white. It fit well and made me look as sharp as a freshly stropped straight razor, but it just did not suit me. I ended up with a thin-striped blue and white sport coat. It fit just fine. When I looked in the mirror, all I could see was Daddy and Shorty setting on Grandmother's porch or out under the willow tree wearing them seersucker suits. Man, I looked good!

Isn't it funny how we full grown-up men still do what our fathers and family did? I think that memories of little things like a seersucker suit can make me stop and chuckle. Today, when I do book signings I wear that seersucker sport jacket. Daddy and Uncle Shorty would be happy and get a chuckle seeing me. When Miss Gail and I got married, Woolf (this is my brother Melvin Oakley) said, "I bought a new sport coat for your wedding. Sorry, but I could not find a seersucker one anywhere." Yes, we do what our father did.

Just Another Hair Cut

So far in this life I, guess that I have had at least a thousand haircuts. If all goes according to my plan, I may get at least another thousand. That is my goal anyway. Through the years, I have never been what you would call vain about my hair. It grows and I get it cut. But I will admit that today, I do keep a careful eye on it, since it has started to turn gray and turn loose. Today, I do investigate my barber just a little. I ask things like their name and have they ever cut hair before — ever?

My earliest remembrance of getting my hair cut was setting on an orange crate in Mr. Sam Smith's tool shop. It cost my father a quarter. Me, Uncle Shorty, Daddy and Arnold would walk over to Sam Smith's every once in a while to catch up on the local news. On some of these walks, we would get our hair cut. Mr. Smith had pretty much one style of cut. "Just hold still while I get that stuff off-n your head," he would say. The barber shears made eight or ten trips across my head, and he got all of the hair off, right down to the bare white skin. My only memory of Arnold is him saying, "No he ain't cutting my hair like that anymore." I think Arnold was big enough to go to high school and needed his hair cut in a more stylish way. You know, something like a "flat-top" or trimmed into "ducktails."

There were boxes of things setting around to play with. I was always fascinated by the old alarm clocks in a box. Also, Mr. Smith had piles of handsaws. He would cut hair until there were no more heads left, then it was time to just talk. He'd talk and sharpen handsaws for people. Daddy said, "Sam Smith would do about anything for a nickel."

Once in awhile, we would go to Colman Hilton's for a haircut. He was a fast trimmer, too! I don't think he or Mr. Smith ever had any barber training. They just took up the trade.

One day Daddy announced that Mason Williams had moved into the "Buster Bryant" house. He can cut hair too." Everyone was pleased. Me, I was happy. Mason Williams had the very first barber chair I had ever seen. Bold as brass setting out there on the front porch, it was. I liked to go up there and get in the chair and pump the handle to raise myself up. I thought that I was in high cotton doing that. Later Mason built a small barbershop near his house and moved the chair into the new shop. I got my hair cut in that shop until I left the country for Rhode Island.

In Rhode Island I got my hair cut by a Chinese man who could only say $2.50. He spoke those words as clear as deep spring water. He could not say any other American words. Just "$2.50."

Even when I moved to West Tennessee, I got my hair cut at one place and then another. When I moved back to Virginia I kinda stopped at the first place I was at when I needed a haircut.

But that all changed when I started to look after my hair a little more. I had been asked to be the commencement speaker at one of the local elementary schools. So I had my best blue suit freshly dry-cleaned and went into town to get a new hair cut. I had been asked to go to the new barber in town.

His place of business was a motel room. This fact should have run up a red flag, but it did not. When I entered the room, it was dark and smelled of stale beer and freshly smoked cigarettes. This should have run up second red flag, but again it did not. When the barber opened the front door real wide to let in some more light I noticed two or three bourbon bottles on the floor. Red flag number three should have run up before my eyes. But again, it did not.

Well, I went on in and just set down in the barber chair. Damn, I should have took to running. The man looked like he was just skin loosely draped over some bones. His face looked like it had worn out two or three bodies. He shook out the apron out over the second floor railing and started coughing like he was going to die. He had a real angry sore on his forehead like he had been fighting with a wild cat and lost. Well anyway, he wrapped the apron around my neck and pulled out a set of clippers. They ran slowly and would not reach top cutting speed. They just would not wind up. "I have got a second set of clippers around here somewhere," he announced. In a minute he came back with a newer looking set of hair clippers and went to cutting. These, thank goodness, would wind up to top speed. His barber skills were a lot like Sam Smith's and Mason Williams'. About all he was interested in was getting the hair off my head.

"Want your mustache and beard trimmed?" he asks. (These were the only words he had said directly to me up to this point.)

"Go on and trim both of them," I mutter. "Keep in mind, I do not want to lose that Sean Connery look of mine. Everyone can see that we look a lot alike."

He starts on my mustache and his feet get caught in the electrical wire on the clippers. He almost stumbles into my lap. He squeaks a little, "Oh, shit."

I holler "Oh, Shit."

Both of said the same thing, but we had a very different meaning. That little rascal stumbled and cut one half of my mustache off my lip. I jumped up and cut the light on and looked in the mirror. Yes, half of it was gone.

There just would not be time to grow another mustache. I had to make my presentation in two days. I stop at another barber shop on the way home and ask them if they would give me another trim and make me look better. "OK," the lady says, "why didn't you come over here first? I cut hair for the football coach, so you know I can cut hair pretty good."

"Yes, ma'am. I will come back, if you can just help me out of this jam."

"Well, there ain't any way to grow that hair back. I will just have to cut the other side off, too."

The day of the school commencement comes. I go and make a wonderful presentation, if I must say so myself. I seems like every eye in the place is focused on me. "Now I have their attention," I think. Not really, I know it is that half-trimmed and half-cut mustache and my lopsided hair that kept their attention. Why did I ever go to that barber? Why, he would not have made a good-sized pimple on the ear of a barber and that is the lopsided truth.

The Man

As a little fat boy growing up on the ridge I was always getting into one thing and another. Trouble was my middle name. Every once in awhile, I would start to get under my Grandmother's skin and she would get a little upset with me. I could always tell this because of an expression she would use. "If you don't slow down and get control of yourself, I am going to call the man. He will come right to this house and haul your little self off and that will be the end of you and that will be that."

Did I think that I was going to be hauled off? Well, the answer is NO. I knew that I was a fixture right there on River Ridge. I was just like them yellow River Jack rocks. I started out here, and here I was going to stay. But there always was a sense of seriousness in tone and a hard look in her face. I just shut up and moved on.

When I was about ten or eleven, I asked about "The Man." The only answer I ever got was, "Well, he is a government man. He comes out into the mountains and looks for young men and women that don't seem to fit anywhere. You know the kids that make trouble and always argue back. He loads them into his real shiny big car and takes them off somewhere. Their parents and grandparents haven't got anything to say about this. They are just gone. One day, sometimes a year or two later, they are returned back to where they used to live. They are different. They are all calmed down."

Uncles Shorty, Nelson and Lake just looked at each other after this statement. Their answer did not explain much of the meaning of the "The Man," but I started to think he was real and that was about all the adults knew of this person and that was all they were going to tell.

After awhile, I just let the man slide back into to my forgotten memory. One day, around my 60th birthday, a person gave me a copy of a book titled *War Against the Weak: Eugenics and America's Campaign to Create the Master Race*, written by Edwin Black. I do think that I am most unqualified to give a complete synopsis of the book. "I find it most difficult to read, but cannot put it down for long periods of time," Charles Lytton.

Early on in the book, statements are made about the Montgomery County sheriff tracking down and catching people on Brush Mountain and transporting them to Western State Hospital in Stanton. There these "hillbillies" or so called "feebleminded" people were deemed insane and were systematically sterilized. (Page 4). "Lower-class white boys and girls from the mountains, from the outskirts of small towns and big city slums, were sterilized in assembly line fashion." (Pages 4 and 5)

After reading part of *War Against the Weak*, I started to think back to the blank look on Nelson's, Shorty's and Lake's faces. They, like many others up the ridges and across the valleys, knew exactly what Grandmother meant by "I will call the man." Only by the grace of God were my uncles and aunts not carried off. Possibly, it was because of the 35 acres of farmland. Each man worked daylight to dark and paid taxes, too. They even went to the elementary school in Long Shop.

As I set here and think back on this subject, I can remember statements about some the older people that I knew. One comment sticks in my mind: "Old Kittle Head has got himself a new wife. The man brought her over a few years ago, and she has done been cut [castrated or neutered] and everything." Again, I had just forgotten this until I got to writing on this section. So these people did live and many of these atrocities happened.

I sometimes still get confused about the "good people" that make the decisions for the rest of us. The "good people" possibly thought that they were doing something real noble and important for the betterment of society. I wonder.

Strong Pee-ers

I just never thought that pee would be such a conversation starter. For once this story does not come from our family. But in some ways it goes to show that a lot of people were a lot like us. I think that True Red-blooded Appalachian Men just went out of their way sometimes looking for humor. Often they found it in the most unlikely of places.

At a recent book-signing, a fellow walked up to me and stated that he had never peed out of a tree onto a train, (that was the subject of one of my stories in an earlier book), but as child he almost peed over the hood of a 1950 Oldsmobile Delta 88!

When the man I was talking to was about five years old, his father bet a dollar that his son could pee farther than any other five-year-old. Another man stepped forward and offered up a one dollar bet on his son. The second father suggested that the boys not pee for distance, but see who had the ability to pee over a car hood. In the parking lot sat a 1950 Oldsmobile. You know, one of them real fast cars. So the two boys were stood side by side and told to pee over the car hood. A whole crowd of men came out of the store to watch the pee contest. Everyone was hooting and laughing. Few had ever seen anything like this before.

"I built up as much pressure as I could and let it fly," the storyteller explained. "I peed over the hood, but I just did not have the pressure to pee all the way over the car. I almost did it; my pee came down on the opposite fender. I won; the other kid only peed as far as the Olds hood.

I would just love to have seen the competition and fathers cheering their sons on. Only on River Ridge! Also, I do not think that peeing will ever make it to the Olympics.

Waiting a Lifetime for my Inheritance

My dear old mother was only a few weeks before death. I kind of knew her death was near, because she was giving away some of her most prized things. She and I just retold all the old stories. We even concentrated hard on remembering people that we did not even know and what had become of them. "Well if we can't remember them people, they are just forget souls," Mom would say.

One afternoon, Mom got kind of quiet and then said to me: "I have a little something I want to give you. Why, don't we call it your inheritance?"

Oh boy, here it comes. I just knew that Mom had squirreled away some money or a real hard diamond or something. She was always tighter than Dick's hatband. I just knew what was coming.

At age 90, Mom walked very slowly. She got up out of her wheelchair and limped over to a small dresser and retrieved a tiny box. It had a little jingle about it as she sat down hard on the bed beside me. I thought, big bills don't take up much space. A key to a safety deposit box might jingle some, too. She said, "Here is something I want you to have." And as I opened the box she added, "None of the others wanted any part of this, but I knew that you would want them."

Now, very reluctantly I opened the box, and there were three little objects. One was a very small glass shoe, made like those once made of wood in Holland. The other two objects kind of took away my breath. I discovered that I had inherited her two kidney stones.

"I want the kidney stones made into a pair of earrings. I think that they would be great conversation-starters. I can just bet that few people have ever seen a 'Stag Horn Kidney Stone.'"

"You are right about that," I replied. "That is the kidney stone that just about killed me a few years back."

I started to laugh. I think that we laughed for hours.

The glass shoe I keep setting in a flowerpot and chuckle each time I water the jade plant. As for the kidney stones, I thought that I had lost the little box, but a little while back I was looking for an important document and I found the kidney stones again. I started to laugh uncontrollably.

At times like these, I wish I had held onto the little jar that held my tonsils. I asked Mom, "Why in the world did you and Dad bring that little jar of tonsils home from the hospital?"

"Well," she said, not one bit edgy about it, "when people ask, 'Did they take out his tonsils?' I would just show your little jar. That was proof positive that they were gone. No need to always be showing people your throat."

If I had the little jar, I could set it right next to the box. I may not have inherited money, or a place on the French Riviera, or even a motor home; but I sure did inherit something that I will remember forever. Memories are good things.

A Walk to the Train Station

As a child on River Ridge, I looked upon everything as entertainment. About everything I saw was fun. In the cool days of early fall and late spring, one of the things that I did for entertainment was to walk to the old train station at Whitethorne. I liked the walk along the river and sound of the trains.

When I was younger I just took these walks for granted. I guess I always thought that the old road all covered in leaves and sticks and the old station would always be there. I would take out down the path by Uncle Shorty's barn and wind around Uncle Nelson's hog pen and slowly walk through May's Hollow. Then I would follow the old road up over the knoll across the railroad and along the river to Whitethorne and on to the train station.

I always thought that it was fun to set in the station on the shiny smooth benches. There were four benches, one each wall. The middle of the waiting room was open. The benches were worn smooth by many butts waiting for passenger trains so long ago. Now they were often covered with dust, because of lack of use. Few people ever came to the train station except me. Oh, there were a few older men who had once either lived along the railroad or had worked on the section crew setting in the old station. They all chewed tobacco and spit into the warming stove just passing the time of day. I do wish that I had taken the time to listen better and try to remember better. Their stories were of interesting people and interesting happenings long ago.

I do not think that I ever saw a train stop for passengers or a person waiting to get on a train. If a train had stopped, I would not have known what to say or do.

But, here I was. I just loved the smell of the place. In the winter the old wood stove was always going. The stationmaster and I talked just a little. He was always talking on the phone, making ready to shift the rail switches or hanging messages on a small clip perched eight to ten feet above the ground. These were messages for the train's engineer. He just did not have much time for me.

One day the stationmaster told me, "The old train station is going to be torn down, and new automatic switch is going to be installed." In less than a year, the old station was just gone. Soon the old road along the river was nothing more than a walking path. By the time I made it to high school the path too was gone. I guess that is what they called "progress."

A short while back I asked Aunt Edith about the old train station. She said it was a happening place when she was younger. People gathered there and visited and talked. She also confirmed one of the stories of Whitethorne my father recounted. Daddy said that there were two hotels, a boarding house, ten or more houses along the road and a large open area with short grass. This was the place where men and women gathered to play croquet. Aunt Edith said that she did not think all of that was true.

I think there may not have been but one hotel, and the other large building was a boarding house. Men working on the farms and railroad lived in the boarding house Monday through Friday and rode the train home on Saturday.

The Coon Hunt

Up on Strobes' Creek

When I was a teenager, fun was the only thing I ever thought about. A young man living down the road from me got his driver's license. That was something that I hoped I would get soon, but at that point Dane had his, and I enjoyed climbing into this little car and riding. I did not care one whit where the car was going; I just wanted to go, too.

One evening about dark, Dane stopped by my house and beeped the horn. I was out the front door and in his little car so fast that it made Daddy's head swim. I found three others and one real big hound in the car. We were going coon hunting. Well, there were few things that I liked more than coon hunting. The four of us rode the back road over the Price Mountain all the way to the creek.

Dane drove his small car right to the water's edge and asked, "Do you think that we can drive across the creek?" For once I kept my mouth shut. I had not been on this stretch of this very small creek, but it did look to be deeper than normal. It had been raining. Someone said, "What is the worst thing that can happen? We could get stuck and have to walk out." Today, I think back and say to myself this was very good insight into the situation. Common sense dictated that we start the coon dog up the creek and see if he struck a coon.

We did not do this. No, Dane put the little car in gear and slowly started across the creek. Within ten seconds the car stopped and water started to come in around the doors. The water was so high up on the doors that I could not push the passenger side door open. While we were talking about our situation, the big dog from the back seat jumped out the window and took off running. I reckon the dog was growing tired of being trapped with a bunch of young fools. Within the next second, I went out the same window. I landed in water about three feet deep.

Everyone followed with the exception of Jacky Lee Jones. He jumped out of the window and in mid-air reversed his body and landed on top of the car.

"How in the world did you get up there?" we asked.

"I have no clue. I just did not want to get my new penny loafers wet," he answered.

We started walking for home. Dane just kept saying, "Daddy is going to kill me deader than a skunk in the road."

Well, after midnight a fellow from up near Prices Fork came by. When he stopped, he asked if the car in the creek was ours and told us the water had gone down and the car would now come out. "If-n you want, I will pull you to Prices Fork."

So we load in the truck and go back to the little car. It was now almost setting on both creek banks with the stream running under it.

With in an hour we are standing at Prices Fork watching Dane enter the telephone booth to call his father to come get him and the car. When Mr. Hutcheson saw the car and us and heard the story, he turned many shades of red. He did think for a minute, but then started to scream at all of us. He was about as mad a person as I have ever seen. I think it even made him mad to carry us boys home.

No the car was not ruined. It just needed an oil change and the distributor dried off. Within two months, you could set on the seats without getting your ass wet. As for the dog, no one actually remembers picking him up; no one ever saw him again either. Coon hunting was just something we boys from River Ridge did for entertainment.

I still see Dane every once in awhile. He said he never went coon hunting again.

The World of Work

One of the most stressful times in my life revolved around Daddy almost being laid off from the Radford Army Ammunition Plant. He had been employed there for as long as I could remember. There had been lots of layoffs and hiring sprees. Thankfully, I was young and did not know or understand what was going on.

When I was about ten years old, my family was going through a very tough time. Every evening when Dad came home, Mom would look at him with big questioning eyes. Daddy would start through a story of who got laid off and who had seniority to bump a person out of a job. Mamma would talk about going back to work at the sewing factory in Christiansburg; that is, if they were hiring.

"There are 19 people with less seniority than me. I can be laid off any day now."

"Is there any job that you can bump into?" Mom would ask.

"Nothing has been posted as yet, and I truly don't want to

bump any man out of his job," Dad would answer.

"I can just bet you that another man will bump you, if it comes down to that. Elmer, you have got to think about your family and us."

That summer we canned everything that we could find. Grandmother's cellar was filled with jars of jelly, green beans, greens, tomatoes, grape juice, applesauce and peaches. "We need to put up everything we can; never know when these foods we will be all we have." When Mom said this, I think it settled in on me that our life just might get hard.

Seemed to me that Daddy would drink a little more moonshine during these times. Mom seemed to holler at him a lot more, too. One evening Daddy announced that two neighbors had been laid off, and the list was down to six men ahead of him.

"I just know that tomorrow will be my last day and have no idea where I will find work. Some men are being offered jobs in at the Hurclease Power Plant in Utah."

"What if you are offered a job in Utah? What are you going to say and what will we do?" Mom asked.

That was an evening of hard talking. Me, I just wondered where we were going go to find work. My little nickel and dime jobs just weren't enough to help.

The next day, Daddy was still number six on the list. Paychecks still kept coming in, and we kept canning everything we could. Every day, I helped carry jars to Grandmother's cellar. Slowly but surely, the tension slowed. Life started to get more normal.

One day, Daddy came home about half shot and announced that he was now sixteenth on the list. Ten men were called back to work. Uncle Shorty was in this group. Mom was happy. She did not say one word about Daddy hitting the bottle in the middle of the week. Me, I was so happy that I wasn't helping to can up every slow animal or any plant without too many stickers. We did eat a lot of canned greens beans, tomatoes and drank grape and tomato juice with every meal that winter. But, I did not care too much; we were employed and life was good again!

Me and the High Plains Drifter?

Last night, I watched the movie *8:10 to Yuma* on television. It was the old black and white version, the one with Glenn Ford. When I was about 20 years old, I saw it for the first time. The thing about the movie wasn't the rugged high desert scenery of New Mexico, the tough cowboys, or even the story of the outlaws. I was enamored with the denim jacket that Glenn Ford wore. It was a short waistcoat with buttons up the front. "Damn, I would look good in one of those," I thought.

At the time, there was a Levis denim store in the local mall. I went there the next morning. I was working at the Mick or Mack Grocery Store, so I had money to burn. When the doors opened, I stepped in the store and was almost overcome by the smell of all the blue jeans stacked all the way from the floor to the ceiling. There might have been a little high desert air stirring, too.

I described the Levis jacket and the nice person working there, a young man, just kind of looked at me. After a long while he said, "Wait here, and I will see if we have the style you are looking for." In just a few minutes, the kind young man returned with a jacket that looked just like what I thought Glenn Ford had worn and handed it to me to try on. I can hardly get an arm through the sleeve. The salesman has to hold the cuff while I pull the denim jacket off.

"Well, that is exactly what I want, but I need a larger size," I explained.

"Mr. Lytton, that is a size 52, and Levis does not make a bigger one," announced the salesman.

Stunned, I guessed that I would have to wait a long time for a new Levis denim jacket. Sometime later, I did get my denim jacket at a Sears and Roebucks. It wasn't what I wanted, but it was the best I could do. When I wore it, not one person mistook me for a 325-pound Glenn Ford in a size 54 jacket and with a scruffy beard. The coat had a zippered front, and I think that the zipper was the thing that kept me from experiencing the feeling of the high desert and being a real cowboy. Probably the fact that I was afraid of horses did not help my cause much.

The Chicken's Role
in Sunday Dinner

Times have changed since I was eight years old. Please just read on and you will see what I mean.

I was asked the other day, "Does a chicken try to run off when its head has been chopped off?" If this question had been asked by an 8- or 10-year-old, a sociologist, a social worker and legal counsel would need to be in attendance before it could be answered. In 1958, the answer was simple: "Yes, the animal runs until it runs out of blood."

Not long ago a 40-year-old woman said: "I have lived my whole life in town, and I've never seen a chicken or anything killed. So, can he run off, and how do you stop him?

When I told her we just put him under an old tub so he did not run off into the weeds and die, she just kind of looked at me like I was some kind of chicken killer.

Grandmother would say, "He's running looking for his head. So you hold onto it so he doesn't find it."

I wondered, "What is he going to do, sew it back on?"

"If you just keep a-holt of it, we won't have to find out."

For us, soon after supper on Saturday evening, the big cast iron pot was filled with water, and a big fire was set under the tub. Everyone just went on about feeding hogs, carrying grain to the horses, milking the cows and straining the milk. Right on cue, the water boiled. Uncle Shorty or Daddy would look the chicken flock over and point to a bird. "That one right there; it ain't laying. Catch it quickly before it gets away."

I would fly into my chicken-catching mode. I did not want any of the "chicken house dust" stirred up. That dry shit makes me caught and sneeze. Hold her still unless you want to lose a finger and whop went the ax. In a flash the hen was under the tub.

As soon as no sound could be heard, the chicken was retrieved from the tub and dropped into the waiting hot water. There it set a minute or two. When I pulled it out, I would pull off all the big feathers and about a million little ones. Uncle Shorty would check my plucking job, then drop the bird back in the hot water and swish it around to clean off the skin and revive any unpicked feathers. "Pick a few more of them. If the hen isn't clean, Mamaw will have you back out here with tweezers getting the pin feathers."

After Uncle Shorty declared the chicken plucked clean of feathers, he held it by the feet and waved it through the fire to remove all the pinfeathers. Next, the chicken was butchered on the chopping block and washed in a galvanized water bucket of cold water. "Well, Harmie (I was nicknamed Harmie back then), we have done done our part. Take that bucket into your Mamaw."

"Uncle Shorty said for me to give you this chicken," I'd tell Mamaw before I turned to leave. "He said that our part was done."

"Well his-un might be, but yours ain't," came the answer.

I would have to wash the chicken in cold water three or four times and then hold the dead bird for Mamaw to cut it into pieces for frying.

"Now go get firewood and fill the wood box for tomorrow."

Fried chicken is still part of many Sunday afternoon meals. I guess someone needs to go to Colonel Sanders and get a bucket of chicken with all the fixings. This new life is just great, ain't it? Do, I wish for the good old days? Well, once in awhile on Saturday when things are slow, I think that it's time to kill a chicken for Sunday dinner, and I laugh out loud.

A Little Fat Boy's
Dream of the "Biggs"

Life was just different when I was a kid! For me the world was a much bigger place back in 1960 than it is now. Just before Christmas last year, I was in one of those giant sporting goods stores. As I watched a man about my age and his grandson, I was taken back to a time when I stood in the Western Auto Store in Blacksburg looking right into a new shipment of baseball gloves. I did not have one, and damn, I wanted one! In fact I felt like I needed one, or I just might bust a gut!

In the back of my mind, I just kind of knew that if I could drop about 30 pounds and get about two or three feet taller, I had a future in the Big Leagues. That is, I would be playing on Saturdays in places like Prices Fork, McCoy, Wake Forest, or Tom's Creek. Yes sir, the local boys and men played ball on Saturday and Sunday, and people came from miles around to watch. That surely is what they were talking about when they would say, "The Biggs."

Well, after very carefully picking up each and every glove and looking at the price tag, I picked out a catcher's mitt. You see, I was very round, very, very slow and right gawky, and if I was stationed behind home plate I would not have to move around lot. It was the cheapest one, too.

Back to modern times. As I stood there in the sporting goods store, listening to a little boy talk and plead with his grandfather for this ball glove, I remembered my days as a child. I can just bet this was a grandfather sent out to babysit his grandson while the parents went Christmas shopping. The more I listened, I decided the roles were reversed: the little boy just might have been sent out to grandfather-sit for a little while. Because the little boy just wandered from one ball glove to the next, asking one question after another, and the grandfather followed along answering the questions the best way he knew how. Today, I just know these things. My littler granddaughters are sent out to grandfather-sit me all the time, and I often find that I am in over my head.

The little boy was having a hard time making up his mind on which glove he wanted, and the granddaddy was just talking about when he was little more than a teenager and had played in the local leagues.

"We went everywhere to play; I met people from all over. Why, I can still smell the dust on the field down in Merrimack. Now, if I buy this ball glove for you, are me and you going to play some ball this spring?"

"Well I guess so," the boy replied.

"Why, in my day," said his granddaddy, "about everybody

wanted to be a ballplayer."

The old man was right. Back in 1958 and '59 and '60, at the old stores and gathering places, older teenagers and younger men would talk about hunting, fishing, ladies and baseball all winter. Me, I just took it all in and did not miss a word. Baseball was full-grown man talk, and I liked it. They could hardly wait for the snow to melt and mud to dry up.

Today, as I set and reminisce, my mind drifts off to my days at Prices Fork Elementary School. My right smallish brain started to drift off to the hot sun coming through my third and fourth grade classroom windows. I reckon the mud had dried up, because I could see Barney Clemons out on the Prices Fork ball diamond raking up leaves and picking up pieces of trash blown in during the winter from the snow fence that separated the ballfield from the school playground. He would pull the wooden drag with a little yellow tractor that he got from the Radford Arsenal. It was one of those little tractors used to pull them wagons filled with explosives.

"Yes, spring will be here soon, and another baseball season will be on us!"

Miss Hattie Guinn hollers right loud at me and jolts me away from watching Barney Clemons to the arithmetic problem scratched on the blackboard.

"Well this just might be the year I take to growing up some and stop growing out so much."

I think real hard, and I still cannot answer that arithmetic problem, so Miss Guinn hollers real loud at me some more. But, I don't seem to hear her too much, because I am thinking of the dust on the ballfield. I can almost see the stands full, and everyone is cheering for me as I come charging around third base.

Did I tell you that it was way up in high school before I could even hit the ball? I was still right gawky and clumsy. Hand-eye coordination had not been invented as yet, so I was commonly referred to simply as "clumsier than hell." But until my coordination developed, I was used as baseball finder, and I bravely searched the high weeds for lost baseballs.

In the years between 1955 and possibly 1965, communities had organized baseball teams managed by local people, and the ballplayers came from the localities, too. They all had pretty good uniforms with names of some local store or garage on them. All the players got to wear real baseball cleats, too. When they walked across a concrete sidewalk, there was no mistaking: "There goes a for-real ballplayer. I could tell by the click on the concrete and screaming of mothers telling the full-grown boy/man not to wear them ball cleats in the house."

To me, possibly the best part of the uniform was the baseball caps. Ball players wore the team's hat with pride and a swagger. Also, people supporting their local team wore ball caps. Ball players took special care of the hats, and personalized them in special ways. Some hats sat in a grocery bag behind the back seat of cars, so they would not get lost or mashed when people piled into cars on the way to the game. Players were always kind of dusting them off.

Me, I never once had a hat, and today I often think, "How much I would like to see one of those old hats or uniforms. Somewhere there needs to be a museum for that old forget stuff."

I noticed that baseball players were damn good cussers, too. They were always fixing to "kick somebody's ass" or "sticking the ball into places where the sun never does shine"

I never did get to play baseball. I was too young and far too uncoordinated. But, I did get to go to many of the games. Until I was about 10 years old, I always thought that it was because I wanted to go. Then I put two and two together and learned that Mommy and Daddy just wanted me out from under their feet and off of River Ridge.

Just a little aside. Today, in 2013, there are lots of books about parents that hover over their children. Once in while, there are seminars on how to send your children off to college and almost go with them. Well Ruth and Elmer did not have any of them books; they wanted me gone on Saturday and Sunday afternoons. The longer the ballgame, they happier they were.

On those Saturdays and Sundays, I was sent to the mailboxes with a small metal Coca-Cola cooler filled with an ice tray of ice, a seven-ounce Coke or Seven-Up, a pint jar of water, and two or three peanut butter sandwiches. Often I would pile in the car with Linwood and his friends. Sometimes Mod Snider would take me with him. Or I would ride to and from the games with one of the men from Long Shop.

Daddy and Mom never ever went, but I had to report everything that happened when I got home. Uncle Shorty would go once in awhile, but not very often. Uncle Nelson often went, but I rarely rode with him, because Daddy didn't want me in that car coming home. You just never knew with Nelson whose house you were going to visit after the game. He had a great nose for moonshine and bootleg, and his driving skills went down the more he sniffed the air.

Like I said, I never played baseball, but I did have a very important job, a job that no regular man or boy would do. The first thing I would do when I got to the ballfield is find the best shade and set my Coke cooler down. As the day moved on, the shade moved on too. Down at Wake Forest there was lots of shade. The ball diamond had a ring of bull pines. Everyone was seated up under the pines on one side of the field at the start of the game, and by the time the game was over about everyone would be seated under the pines on the other side. Those people were country astronomers and understood the true meaning of movement of the sun. Me, I just moved with the crowd.

Oh, my job was to track down foul balls and bring them to my team's bench. Now this might sound easy, and most of the time it took only a minute or two, but in some ways it was harder than you think. Tracking foul balls will teach a fat little boy a good bit about poison oak. If a ball stopped rolling in a thick clump of poison oak, I just had to get it out of there. Often I would find a stick and rake the ball back into the grass, but if no stick was around I would just wade right on in.

I was always red from my ankles to my knees and itched from the poison oak. I did not have any long pants to help protect my legs. Mother was still making short britches for me out of cotton feed sacks. The biggest problem with them short britches was they had no pockets, so there was no place to keep my chewing tobacco or cigarettes. If I put either by the cooler, the bigger kids would chew up my Mail Pouch and smoke up my Chesterfields. Most times I just fooled them and left my tobacco at home.

I can still hear the older boys telling me not to pitch the ice from my Coca-Cola cooler. We would be going to Bevan's Store after the game, and we were going in to buy cold beer. It would be put in my cooler. Me, I never got one cold beer, or a warm one, for that matter.

One day I just stopped going to watch baseball. I never went again. I think that the bigger teens discovered girls, and they did not have the time for one fat little boy. Some of the younger adults became fathers, and their lives and priorities changed. Me, I was changing too! I was getting old enough to go to the New River, and my life would never be the same.

Baseball just seemed to end or stop. And I never understood why new younger men and boys others did not show up to replace those that had moved on. Possibly, the communities were changing too. Never again did I see baseball hats in the back windows of car. Was it the television? I was watching more and more "I Love Lucy" and "Bonanza." The New River was also starting to take holt on me, and once the river gets her hands on you she just never does seem turn you lose.

Anything That Floats but Boats

It is the summer of 1973, and I am in my youthful river prime. I am tanned all the way to the tops of my swimming shoes. My hair is kind of long and bushy, and some of the hairs have been bleached kind of red and yellow by the sun. But my most impressive feature is my belly tooting out like a morning glory. Yes, I am a true Appalachian American specimen. Jay and Gary arrive at the cabin. One of them announces that there is a group of people leading a road rally from Roanoke to the Junction. The Junction is a small park on New River, downriver from McCoy. "They are having a anything that floats — other than boats — race. Anybody can join in." someone explains. "If we went for the race, what would we paddle down the river?"

There were a few old boards out there by the barn, but they would never do. There was an old refrigerator, but most likely it would just sink. Why don't we go up to Pride Arrington's and cabbage off one of those fiberglass concrete forms? Great idea, we all agree.

When the coliseum at VPI was built, more than 100

fiberglass box-shaped concrete forms were used. After the concrete was poured, the forms were given to Pride Arrington, who sold them to local framers to use as feed boxes. Well, all except one. We climbed over the fence, slid on over into the road and pushed it into the back of my truck. This was all done in a coordinated fashion in the blink of an eye. In my truly small mind, I thought, "Why ask for something or purchase something when you and two buddies can steal it?" I was right happy about our morning effort. The plan for the anything-that-floats-but-boats race was coming together.

We stop at Long Shop Grocery and purchase one or two cartons of Blue Ribbon beer and start toward McCoy. On the way, we are passed by a few strange cars; some have very weird watercraft on top. So the road rally part of the day must be drawing to a close and the "anything but boats" part is starting soon. We arrive just in the nick of time. People are putting every kind of thing in the water, but there is nothing as water-worthy as our concrete form. So we pitch the thing in the water and join the crowd headed for the falls. Most of the crafts just disintegrate within a few minutes. Our form is not leaking too awful much, but it takes on some water each time we lean over the sides to paddle. This truly is a great craft to get one or two, possibly even three people drowned. But on we go.

The remaining contestants pull over to the side just before the falls. Everything is put on the back of trucks and transported back to the Junction. We all get to be friends very quickly. We are so friendly, in fact, that I give my truck keys to total strangers and they use my blue truck to help carry watercrafts back to the Junction.

When we arrive at the Junction, we put the things back in the water and go down the river a second time. Now we have two paddling and one dipping water fulltime. Down the river we go, and we are making better time than anyone. Country boys take each and every task as if we are playing very seriously and stick with it until all the fun is wrung out of it. When we get back to the Junction another pickup truck is pulling in. People run to the truck like it's full of candy or something.

Everybody just seems to lose interest in the race, and this is just when we are about to show everyone what we are made of. So I drift over to the truck, too. There I see one of the most impressive things I have ever seen!!! The truck has six — yes six — kegs of beer in the back. Them town boys are struggling to get one of them kegs out of the truck. Me, being a full-blooded, 6' 3," 300- pound Appalachian American, I just reach up into the truck and ask them, "Where do you want them kegs?"

I do not think that these new friends of mine were as impressed with me as I was with me, for they just kind of looked at me like, "Where did this true Appalachian specimen come from?" You could see on their faces the question, "Who invited this behemoth of a man? Damn he sure can carry beer kegs, too."

I tell them, "Why, they ain't no bigger than a good-size shoat."

They laugh uncontrollably. "A shoat? What is a shoat?" they ask each other."

In no time at all, six kegs are neatly arranged on a tarp, and lots of ice is piled up on those wonderful containers filled with magnificent amber liquid. I must admit that I was more than willing to lend my back to the task and more than willing to lend my mouth to the tasting of this fine free beer. About all I can think is, "Heaven has done come to McCoy this very day, and I was here to see it!"

Some older lady, maybe 30 years old, (I do not know her name) was very quick to instruct me as to where to put the beer kegs and how to place them. Once I finished, she was also quite sharp and direct on advising me that my services were most appreciated and that I could move on to some other place — preferably another town or even another state, anywhere far downriver would be OK. Well, I just kind of worked my way over to the tall plastic cups and drew me a good cold one and walked down to the river to check out our water craft. I was a true contestant in this here river event, so I had to keep up my watercraft. This here is shaping up to be a great day!

As the day wore on Jay, Gary and me made three or four trips down the river. As I recall, we always were first to take out. I think that we just loved the river and knew how to paddle anything down it. Possibly, town boys or town men were not into paddling at all. Possibly, they had no clue just how good we were. Possibly, they were more into those beer kegs than the race. Well, anyway, as the day wore on, fewer trips downriver were taken and more time was spent with those beer kegs. Damn, life was good.

Another thing, the more we hung around, the more the group seemed to like having us in attendance. Me, I think my role was comic relief. People kept asking me, "How did you get so big and strong?"

I answered, "Good vittles, and I was never put out with what my mother put on the table. Also, I did not get the hind tit, like a lot of other people."

They just laughed and gave me another cup of beer.

Yes, I was just stupid, and they knew it. I just did not catch on for a few years. Today, I would like to meet up with this bunch and talk. I wonder what we would say to each other.

Music in the Dust

I think that I need to tell you that Auber Sheppard asked me write this story. So here goes.

It was a very hot summer afternoon. Chuck Shorter and me have been in the hayfield for a few days, and the first cutting of hay has been pitched into the barn loft at the farm on Toms Creek and Prices Fork. There is just one large load of hay left. It is resting on Chuck's old red GMC. We are scheduled to deliver it to Riner the next morning.

Chuck and me are kind of celebrating the fact that the first cutting is in the barn. We are all reared back on his front porch. We each have a bottle of store-bought bourbon. We are just counting cars like Uncle Nelson, fighting the gnats and enjoying the light, cool breeze under in the shade of the big maples. David Price and Aubrey Sheppard drive up. They get out of David's pickup and walk over real quiet like and set down. They pick out a bottle and take a long, soothing draw of bourbon. Yes, life of country boys is simple, but harder than Chinese arithmetic to explain to one of those people from town!

After a few minutes of talking about the virtues of store-bought bourbon, cool shade and hay, David asks Chuck if he could purchase that load of hay. Now, there are a few strings attached to this sale. First off, we have got to go help him unload the hay into this barn. Chuck tells David that this load of hay has been promised to a person in Riner. Then the bottles are passed around another time or two. As the volume of bourbon goes down, so does Chuck's resolve to sell this hay in Riner. Before you know it, we load up in the old GMC and start out for David's barn.

Here is where it starts to get a little fuzzy. We back up to the barn, and I start pitching the hay through the small door into the loft. But the pickup truck does not show up until we are just about finished. David and Aubrey have made a run to the liquor store in Blacksburg. They return with two or three new bottles of liquor.

Aubrey said it was Jack Daniels. Me, I do not remember the brand. Hell, who cares. It was all good back then.

We walk over to David's house, but his wife is sick, so we just do not want to bother her. David does slip in and get his guitar. We start looking for another place to go and resume our leisurely evening. As dark falls on us, we end up at the wide spot at Keaster's Branch.

I can remember the sound of the small stream as the water tumbled over the rock. I also can remember the sound of David's guitar and picking and singing. We all huddled under the bed of Chuck's big GMC. When cars would past, I can remember the road dust being almost trapped under the truck bed.

We sat there on the good, clean dirt and enjoyed each other's friendship and the slow burn of high-dollar bourbon going down our throats. Cars passed, the dust picked up and settled again and again. The music seemed to get better as time passed. After awhile, a few low-hanging thunder clouds crossed over Keaster's Branch, and a very slow rain started to fall, but we were mostly dry up under the truck bed. "Well, the dust is gone for a while," we said.

Before you know it, the 11:45 p.m. whistle in the Radford Arsenal blew over the ridge. In just a little while, the midnight whistle blew as the shifts changed. All good things do come to an end. So we all loaded up and headed for home. When I got to the cabin, I discovered that I was covered from head to toe in a one-drop-thick layer of mud. About the only thing that I recognized of me was the whites, or reds, of my eyes. I went outside and stripped and had to take a bath before I could get in the bed. The next morning, I had to wash the seat of my pickup, because it was covered in a layer of dried mud.

Sometimes fun comes at a price. The truth of the matter is, I had almost forgotten the wonderful evening. Thank goodness for friends like Aubrey Sheppard! Sometimes the pure pleasure and gift of friendship can only be measured by sweat, the thickness of mud and a few bottles of bourbon. Yes, country boys are a simple lot. Thank you for remembering.

Rural Electrification

I cannot remember ever a time when we did not have electricity in our house. I can remember the one light bulb, hanging down from the center of the ceiling at Grandmother's. There was a long string hanging down a few feet, which was used to turn it on and off. This was the way it was until I was maybe about 9 or 10 years old.

Uncle Lake, Uncle Shorty, Daddy and Uncle Nelson and possibly Great Uncle Delmer gathered at Grandmother's for a few long weekends. The purpose was to improve the electric and wiring in The House. [Grandmother's house was call "The House," and everyone in the community knew her home as "The House."] Holes were knocked in the plaster walls of "The House" and holes drilled through the wall studs. Wires were pulled in every direction. A big fusebox was nailed up on the wall of the front porch. New ceiling lights were affixed to the ceiling. Along the walls, electrical outlets were added —one or two outlets per room.

At the time I did not think much about it. Today, I think about it. I can bet that Grandmother started housekeeping in "The House" with brand new kerosene lamps and was happy to have them. Later, with rural electrification, a new lightbulb was attached to a long wire hanging from the ceiling, and again she thought "Will wonders never cease?" Then one day, her children came to "The House" with a big roll of wire. Now, no one had to stand on a chair and unscrew the lightbulb and screw in the electric plug to listen to the radio or plug in new electric appliances or plug in the television. I can only imagine the change that my grandmother experienced.

Maybe I write to record the changes that I have seen in trips across this fine planet. Television, self-winding watches, ballpoint pens, the Internet, embryo transfer in cattle, sugar diabetes — the list goes on.

Sometimes the Things You Do as a Kid Stick with You

Some things are just part of who I am. As a child and teenager, I was regularly sent to the edge of Mr. Luther's fields and to the lot beside the barn to pull what Daddy called "bull weeds." As he explained it: "Hogs have a need for green things to eat. They might even catch the scurvy if they don't have green weeds to eat."

Often he would launch into stories about sailors lost at sea for weeks, months and even sometimes years. Daddy told me over and over that they found they almost always had the scurvy and how they just wanted some green vegetables to eat. Today, I know these weeds as goldenrod, lambs' quarter, giant ragweed and common ragweed.

Our hog lot was bare earth with not one green sprig of grass. Often, you could see the hogs setting down, looking at a clump of earth and waiting for a blade of grass or a weed seed to germinate. As soon as the little sprig of green appeared, they would eat it. Generally speaking, hogs were killed in the fall, so the hog lot lay fallow all winter and spring. Tall weeds and grass would grow and cover the hard-packed earth. In the early summer, Daddy would buy three of four shoats, and in a matter of days all the weeds were either eaten or trampled under the hogs' feet.

So now the hogs were needing something green to munch on. You know, the threat of scurvy and all. Me, I think it was kind of boy-training — helping me to become a strong teenager. Possibly, helping to improve my chances of becoming a man. No, I think it was just something to keep me busy. If I was pulling weeds for a few hours, I was out from under everyone's feet at the house. You guessed it: I was now back in the weed-pulling business. I found that hogs will eat about any weeds except stickweeds and thistles. They aren't much on leaves, either.

About two or three times a week, I was dispatched to the weed patch to pull weeds for the hogs. Finding weeds wasn't hard at all. They grew about everywhere inside the fence rows, in potato patches and around the gardens. Out in the pasture, a good-tasting weed did not stand a chance. The cows and horses saw me looking for a weed, and they ran over to the easy ones and ate them before I could get there.

Well anyway, in the early summer I could easily pull a few armfuls of weeds and pitch them over the fence into the hog lot. The pigs would jump and run; I must admit I enjoyed watching the happy hogs play and eat. By late summer the hogs had done eaten the easy-to-find and easy-to-pull weeds.

They had eaten all the mature pea and green bean vines from all the gardens, yet the search for weeds went on.

Often the "bull weeds" were now taller than me, with massive root systems. I simply could not pull them. When I told Daddy about my problem, he said, "If-n I was you, I would quit trying to pull them weeds and start using a corn-cutter to chop them down." Every time I would chop into the big weeds, I would be covered with orange pollen. Sometimes I could shake the plants and let the pollen ride the wind down over the hill away from me. So I took to chopping an armful about every day and carrying them to the hogs. Hogs just loved to eat the flowers from the weeds. This went on until fall, when the weeds died.

Now, here is where it gets a little funny. Some might say this is a bit sad, but everyone will agree that they will need to shake their heads a little at me after reading this. Last summer, I started walking in the Town Park. It was once a large dairy farm. There are mowed walking paths all over the park. Then about September of last year, I came up on one of the biggest patches of "pig weeds" I have ever seen. There were "pig weeds" much taller than my 6'2" frame. They were thicker than the hair on Old Goldie's back. I just waded out into them, and the sky turned kind of orange from all the pollen I knocked free.

I coughed, sneezed and wheezed. But I just kept walking. I thought, "Fifty years ago, where were all of these "bull weeds" when I needed them?" I then laughed out loud, "Hell, if Daddy had known about these weeds, he would have wanted me to walk up here and pull at least two large armfuls every day.

When I laughed, I heard a person say, "Are you ok? What are you doing in those weeds? You are supposed to stay on the mowed walking path."

When I told my story, the man looked at me like a stillborn calf or something. "Don't you know those big weeds will make you sneeze" he asked.

Well, I do now. I did not tell him that I learned about ragweed pollen and allergies more than 50 years ago. There was no need to talk any more. You see. he was a fullgrown town person, raised on already sliced bacon and canned hams that came from Piggly Wiggly or Kroger's Store, and not from a hog that had ate bull weeds. I could tell that he had never once been sent in search of "bull weeds" to keep hogs happy and scurvy-free. Some things are just ingrained into a person, and they stick with you all of your life, like it or not. I am a true weed-puller.

Sled Riding

We had our first snow of the winter this week. Schools were closed. It took hours before the plows came through the community. I got out early after the snow stopped falling to clean off the driveway. I wanted to see my friends and talk about the big snow. I wanted to see the kids all bundled up headed for "Killer Hill." I wanted to remind them to close the gates as they entered the farm. I wanted to encourage them to pull each other around for a few minutes to clean the rust and film from their sled runners. I wanted them to ask me to join them. I wanted to tell them that tonight when the roads freeze back, their sleds would hum like jar flies on the hard top.

I shoveled my driveway and cleaned out around a few of my neighbors' cars, and no kids came to sled ride. So after a while, I just went back in the house and set down and drank my own hot chocolate and coffee and wished for a day or two of youth!

When I was a little boy, I just loved sleigh-riding. I get

caught up in remembering and writing about this, and I just start laughing out loud. I had an old sled with no lever in the front for steering. To steer, I had to be lying down on my stomach with hands on the runners. I pulled to the left or right to steer. It was slow on the short runs, and it was one of a kind, but I liked it. Given a long run, the thing would get to going so fast that it would almost come off the ground. No other kids ever wanted to ride it, because it was frightfully heavy and a bear to pull back up the hills.

One time, I came off the hill by Uncle Shorty's barn. I was headed for the pond. It was early in the morning, and I was going to chop a hole in the ice for the horses and cows to drink through. I was laying on the old heavy dull ax. Down over the hill I came. This was not such a steep or long hill, but it was all ice. In a second or two, the ride was over. I went across the old pond dam and ran headlong into a big black willow tree. I was knocked out colder than a cucumber for a few seconds. When I woke up, all I could think of was the ax. It was far down below the willow tree. I chopped the holes in the pond and started the hard walk back up the hill. About all I could think of was, "Well I made it again, and wonder how long my luck is going too hold out?" I just never could think about how fast I was going or how much fun it was to go fast.

Possibly, that sled was so damn ugly and worn-out the no one wanted to be seen on it. I also pulled coal buckets from the coal pile to the house on it. I pulled sacks of corn feed to the hog lot and slop buckets from our house and Grandmother's on the old sled. Spilt pig slop may have encouraged others not to ride it. It was often wet and stunk of sour hog slop.

My old sled, she was ugly, but there were worse ones out there. There was a family down the road that took sheets of tin and nailed one end to a telephone pole and bent it into a carved shape, then pulled out the nails. They had made themselves a homemade toboggan. The tin sled would go fast, but if you did not wear thick leather farm gloves, you could easily get a finger cut off. Me, I have also gone down many a hill in a cardboard box. They, too, will go fast, but you need to be ready for the box to decelerate and force you to make the remainder of the ride on your butt.

When I was 10 or 12, I thought that I was big stuff. The first time I went to Prices Fork to sled ride, it was not more than four miles from my back door to the fire barrel on the hill behind Grats' Store. Sometimes I walked the whole way. Once in awhile, someone would pick me up and give me a ride. On this hill is where the big kids and cool people went sled-riding. There was an old 50-gallon metal barrel on top of the hill, with a big fire made in it to warm up your hands and feet.

The hill was long, and there was a small, shallow ditch at the bottom. But this was never much of problem. There were a few moderate-sized locust trees down from the ditch, and there was a wire fence right at the bottom. When you went down over the hill, you had to be thinking about these three things: ditch — trees — fence.

I did not take my old sled up to Grats' Store. Never know, they just might not have let me go down over their hill on such a contraption. I rode down the hill on a big Coke sign or car hood. Either would hold five or six people. After a few trips, the snow got packed down hard, and the downhill run was as fast as a bullet. The faster the tack became, the more you had to make sure you were thinking about those three things; because as you got closer to the trees or fence, you had to jump off. The hard-packed snow would almost rub the meat off of your hands and blind you with snow and ice as you plowed through it.

Every once in awhile, I or we would stop thinking about these important things. Once. we forgot to jump off the Coke sign before we got to the trees. We were going so fast that we went between two close trees. The sign closed up like a clam shell and sprung back out to its original shape with a bang after we cleared the thicket. No one was hurt or even scratched. We did jump before the fence.

The best ride of all just might have been an old Plymouth car hood. More people could ride that than the Coke sign. It went fast. We would pass people walking back up the hill like they were standing still. The Coke sign and the car hood had one interesting feature in common: YOU could not steer them at all. Them things just went where they wanted to go. You could see the ditch coming fast and you just could not steer away from the bump. When we would go through the ditch, half of the riders would be thrown off. The other half just held on for dear life. Screams of laughter were heard from both groups.

For every fun thing there is in the world, there is something not fun at all. We had to walk back up the hill through the deep snow. The Coke sign and car hood had to be pulled, too. By the time I made it back to the fire barrel, I was sweating like a hog — yes, a hog, not a pig. Boys and girls alike had small white columns of steam rising off their heads a foot or so into the frozen air. It was very pretty there in the moonlight and starlight by a big fire. Warm our hands and feet some, and we'd be ready for another try at the hill.

I can remember being almost sad when it can time to head for home. To my house on River Ridge was about a five-mile walk. Often I would be on the road by the time the midnight whistle blew for the shift change at the Radford Arsenal. Almost always someone would pick me up and give me a ride home. The driver and riders would tell me stories of their youth sled-riding on cold, snowy nights. They told me things like how pretty the girls were, and no matter how thick their coats were you could always see the girl beneath. The smoke could not hide the smell of their perfume. They would start to laugh out loud and tell of other youthful stories. Once in a while, the men would start talking about men and women, and tell stories from their youth. These people they spoke of were too old and too straight-laced to have ever been young and surely could not have done such things. I just listened in wonder.

Every now and then, no ride came, or one was late in coming. I would walk as quickly as possible down the road. In the cold night air, I would think of ghosts reported to move on such nights. The wind just seemed to be lowing right down my thin coat collar, and that made me walk faster. When you're in a group, ghosts never seem to come or stalk you. But on these cold nights with bright stars, they seemed to be about everywhere. When a car finally came, I was so happy that I just sat in the noise and warmth of the heater and could not pay any attention to what the carpoolers were even talking about. Ghosts and haunts just don't hang around where full-grown adults are. I have to admit, I often wondered just how old a boy had to get before the haunts went in search of some other youth.

On rare occasions, I would walk the whole way home. These walks were made quickly, with a long line of trailing ghosts, witches and haunts. But by the time I was old enough to drive the family VW bus, I had lost interest in sleigh-riding. I have no clue where the big Coke Cola Sign or the car hood went. No one goes looking for these things today.

Every once in while, I would take to running up the road and sliding on my shoes. Once, I went 20 or more feet. I got to thinking about a man I once knew who fell and cracked open his head. I stopped my running and sliding. I did not want anyone to see just how small my brains are. If my brains were those big ropey kind, I might not mind too much, but they ain't. So, after a while, I just went back into the house and set down and drank my own hot chocolate and coffee and wished for a day or two of youth! I still love the snow and the cold.

"Killer Hill" just sits very quietly waiting for me to come back. Maybe next snow fall or next winter.

A Real Big Belly Isn't Always Bad

It was early in the winter of my fourth grade year at Prices Fork Elementary School. I am guessing that I was 10 or 11 years old. By now, I was a seasoned well-driller; I had already been working the old machines for two years. I could cuss and smoke cigarettes with the best of them. I would sneak a little nip once in awhile, too. I could do about anything around the old machine that any of the men could do. I had already helped complete two or three wells, start to finish. I was even considering being a well-driller when I grew up. This here was honest-to-goodness real man's work, and I just loved it. I stayed filthy dirty, wet and caked with sweat. I lived on potted meat, Vienna sausages, sardines and Double-Colas. Of course, there were a few saltine crackers eaten, too.

The old machine is set up on blocks in the side yard of my house on River Ridge. It is very cold, so cold, in fact, that the fire barrel is no more than five feet from the well-hole being dug. Holding the guide cable makes my hands freezing cold, and I am always putting my hands over near the heat of the barrel. Both Daddy and Mr. Grissom are greasing and lubricating the old machine. "It is very cold, and the machine is very stiff, so we ran it slowly for a while. It needs time to warm up and limber up some too," instruct both of them.

For about 15 minutes, the machine idles along, then the throttle is pulled wide open, and a thick burst of black smoke shoots out the exhaust pipe. The well-digger resumes its normal sounds and rocking motion, and a loud thud comes when the one-ton drill bit is raised and then dropped deep into the earth.

Everything goes very well for a few hours. On a regular basis, water is poured down into the hole. This acts like a lubricant for the drill bit. About every half hour, the heavy digger is removed from the hole, and a smaller water bailer is lowered into the hole. All of the water that was just dumped is now bailed out. Along with the water come the fragments of dirt and rock broken up by the heavy bit. This goes on through the morning. I tell you this because things can go wrong in a matter of seconds!

I am again guiding the cable to the heavy, one-ton bit, so that it does not erode the top of the hole. I am paying close attention to my job, when all of sudden the digger engine races wide open. The cable in my hand is drawn taut and quivers. I hear a loud crack from something breaking. I look up and kind of lean back a little; my stomach is sticking out. I am hit by something and thrown clean away from the machine. Again, I am knocked out. All this takes no more than a second to happen.

Daddy, Uncle Shorty, Mr. Grissom and Mother are standing over me.   They are asking me questions a mile a minute. I am carried into the house and stripped buck necked right down to the undershorts — undershorts if I had had any on. Even as a youth of 10, I just could not get the knack of that binding garment.

"Where were you hit?   What hit you? Does this hurt?" everyone is asking me.

The large gear from the top of the well-drilling machine had swung around and hit me in the stomach. I was just dazed for a few minutes. No ribs were broken. I was not even cut. Just one long, wide, red scratch on my stomach, and it is puffing up as I am examined. The next day, I had a big black bruise on my stomach, and I was made to wear clean undershorts to school.

"Why?" I asked.

"Because you are going to be showing off that scratch and black knot to everyone who will look at it," answered Mother.

Here is what happened, we think. When we were pulling the big bit out of the well, down deep in the earth, a piece of rock ledge must have broken off and fallen into the well. Most likely, it was resting on top of the drill bit. I wedged against the bit when I started to pull it out. That meant the bit could not be pulled from the well, and it put the well-drilling machine in severe strain. There was no safety override clutch or sheer pin for these situations. So the machine kept on pulling and straining until the top gears broke and came crashing to the ground. The whole action took no more than a second! Well, that is what the grownups said.

Sometimes a second is long, long time. I learned that is plenty enough time to get killed in. Mother wanted me to start keeping away from the machine; but once it was repaired, I was right back in the thick of things. I wanted people to ask me about the boom breaking and then to ask me to show them where the big gear hit me.

Today, I laugh and say to myself "thank goodness" for good luck and big bellies. Once in a while, luck just might be as good a thing as having skill and knowledge. The Good Lord must have something planned for me.

P.S. I kept on working as a well-driller through my sixth and seventh grade years. By high school, Mr. Grissom, Daddy and I were not working the well-drilling machine. Just as well; there wasn't much future in it anyway.

Learning to be Cool

Learning to be a grown-up is harder than you might think. One of the dumbest things I did was plant one of the biggest gardens ever seen on New River. The Johnson grass was and still is a fierce competitor. I would chop weeds all day long on Saturday, and by the next Saturday you could not tell that the garden had once been clean. I had long rows of potatoes; big blocks of red, yellow and pink tomatoes. I had planted so many green beans that me and the deer and rabbits had plenty to eat and share. I also had planted marijuana between most of the tomato plants.

Marijuana was a fast grower; it was even faster than the Johnson grass. I had smoked a little pot, but I just could not get the knack of the stuff. I'm thankful to say it made me sneeze and aggravated my sinuses. Each time I gave it a try, my nose swelled up on the inside like a toad, and I talked real funny. I did save the seeds though, and for some reason I just liked growing it. Possibly, it was like being a moonshiner. I felt like I was getting away with something illegal. Daddy, Shorty and other adults came to the garden for vegetables. They looked at the strange plants, but no one ever asked what they were. Younger people looked at the plants, and they knew what they were! Once in awhile, these younger people would pull up one of the plants and carry it home to dry.

When the plants got about head high, I pulled them up and stored them in the little barn. It is fortunate that I removed them. One day, I came down over the hill, and there was a hell of a commotion. There was a police car and an ambulance. Someone had drowned upriver a few days before. When the body was found, the closest boat landing was beside my garden. Daddy and Mr. Snider and Uncle Shorty sent everyone home with a bag of potatoes and tomatoes. There was truly plenty for everyone. I have always thought that I was just plain lucky that I had pulled up the plants. I do not think that a judge would find it funny that I was watching the plants grow.

Within a few weeks, the marijuana plants were gone. Mice and rats from all over the river came and feasted on them. I just went back to growing fruits and vegetables. They did not make me cough and wheeze like the marijuana did.

You may ask about my drug use. Well, I still liked my nicotine, caffeine and alcohol; they were good enough for my family and they remain good enough for me, too.

I learned to grow up finally. It took awhile, and here I am. I was very cool and ort to be glad. Lesson learned!

An Old Ashtray

One time, I go it in my head that I ort to go to college. Somewhere around 1972, I took myself over to New River Community College and enrolled. I thought that I should take only one class as a way to get myself back in the habit of concentrating. I do not know where I got the idea of "back in the habit of concentrating." I had never studied anything in my life other than possibly the game laws for hunting and fishing. I knew them backwards and forwards. But other subjects in school — well, I had not done to well. Oh, I did graduate, but I kind of got by on my good looks and pleasant manly nature, if you know what I mean. I was right pretty in a rugged way — real rugged.

I enrolled in a first-year college math class. "Surely, if I take only one class, I will catch on right quick on how to be a college student," I am thinking. I am 21 years old and have not had a math class since a General Business Math my sophomore year in high school. I do not remember my letter grade, but I can just bet it was no more than a C or D.

I go buy the textbook and walk up to the library and set down and look the first few pages over. And I am OK. They are not hard at all, and I can even do them without any instruction. Soon, I am in the library looking up the answers in the back of the book. I can use the trial and error method to find out how to work the problems. Not much later, I am in the classroom, and I don't even know how to write the problems on my sheet of paper and have no clue how to solve them. NONE. I can't even go to the student math help center, because I can't even figure out how to ask the question.

I am setting at the cabin one Saturday morning, strong coffee in one hand, a fresh-lit cigarette in the other. The coffee pot is almost empty, and the ashtray is full. I have not slept much for the past two nights trying to figure out how to answer the questions at the end of the chapter. Then, out of the blue, drives up Wimpy Williams.

"Well, do you want to go fishing, or do you want some help?" asks Wimpy. I think that Wimpy almost pulled out his hair trying to teach me freshman algebra. He never did laugh too much, either.

I do say thank you. I did go on and learn how to do algebra, geometry and some physics. I even took a class in calculus. Not because it was required; I just wanted to see if I had gotten any smarter. No, that is not the true reason either; I wanted to test my friend Wimpy's skills. I discovered they were wonderful.

Today, after being a teacher, I encourage youth to always take the hardest kind of math they can. I tell them the story of me and Wimpy. I tell them I just might not be as nice as Wimpy, and I don't think that I am as smart.

I had an ashtray made of cast iron given to me by Mr. Hubert Grissom. When he moved out of the cabin, and I moved in he said, "Well I don't need this anymore, and you might need it."

I did not smoke much, but you never know. I wish I had it today. It was in the shape of VT, the old Virginia Tech emblem. As a child, I knew where Virginia Tech was, but never once did I walk across the campus to even look. In my early years, when I worked at Virginia Tech, I never had the nerve to look around any farther than the farms. The students all seemed to be tall, good looking and smart. A college education was something only my mother wanted, and I had no clue how get one. But along came Wimpy, and he knew how. Thanks again, Wimpy.

My First Wreck

I got my driver's license one day and had my first wreck the next. Me and a friend were driving down the back road from Shelors' Store. I know we were going a little too fast, but in a VW bus you had to go fast down the hills to get up the next hill. That was my thinking anyway. My friend was right behind me in his family's VW bug. We were not racing ,because my family's VW bus would not go fast enough to race. It just would not. I went around the curve just past the Tom's Creek Bridge, and the VW bus leaned over on two wheels. It went possibly 25 yards on two wheels. I jumped from the driver's seat into the passenger seat. I was hoping to shift the balance enough to make the bus come back down on all four tires.

Well, it did not! The VW bus went on and turned over on its side. I fell from the passenger seat onto the driver's side door. The old thing did not slide more than 10 or 15 feet. It was wrecked anyway. My close friend and I just looked the situation over, and there was nothing to do but put the old VW bus back up in its four wheels. To do this, we just got a-holt of the little water gutters on the top and started to lift. In a matter of two or three seconds, we had flipped the van back up on its wheels.

I drove the old van home. Holy Macaroni, there was hell to pay on River Ridge for a few days. Yes, I did learn a lesson. Daddy got the bus repaired, but the lesson has stuck with me to this very day. Once the van was fixed, it was my responsibility to change the oil, keep good tires on the old hack, pay for all repair work and pay the insurance. Yes, it was a good experience. I am a stickler for maintenance and try to be on the lookout for teens that know how to drive but really don't.

Now, you are getting ready to ask me if this is true. Every word. I never even gave one thought to lifting and turning the car back onto its tires. We just grabbed a holt and gave a lift. I think it was one of those times when you get stronger when you get scared.

A Trip Over to Reed Lumber

People were always borrowing Daddy's old 1964 panel wagon. They hauled about everything in it. One day, I had ridden in the wagon over to Reed Lumber with a local fellow. We had worked right hard loading the lumber and stopped at the Bridge Tavern to refresh ourselves for the ride home.

I am no more than 14 or 15 years old at the time, but right on into the Bridge Tavern I went. It was just like the last time I was there. The floor needed to be swept, and the dirty windows needed to be opened to let in some unbreathed air in and some of the cigarette smoke out. Everyone I walked past had real bad breath, too. There was a thick smell of grease from the fried hamburgers in the air.

We sat down in a booth and Sugar Foot ordered a beer, He asked me if I wanted one too. I answered yes, with a big smile. For the next few hours, we sat around and drank draft beer, joined the crowd in smoking cigarettes and ate pickled eggs and greasy hamburgers.

When we got home Sugar Foot and me were both sober, but I was sure that Daddy could smell the beer on my breath and cigarettes on my clothes. He knew in an instant where we had been all afternoon and what we had been doing.

"Damn you, Sugar Foot. Why in the hell did you take him to the Bridge Tavern and get him loaded?"

"Elmer, he ain't loaded. Why, I only gave him 3.2 beer. And besides he was drinking red-eyes," said Sugar Foot.

After that Daddy was OK. He looked at me and asked if I had made Sugar Foot buy my beer and cigarettes.

"No, I spent my own money," I answered. "I don't want to go and start to mooching off-n others."

When I got my driver's license, I felt like I was free to go to the tavern, too. I did this some, but not that often. I was big enough, but I was under-age and Daddy had asked me to not be drinking and driving. "It is best to buy your beer and go to the river and drink it," he admonished. And I did.

The Bridge Tavern is now gone. For that matter, so is Reed Lumber Company, but I think about that afternoon every time I drive past. Just maybe, that was one of my first days being almost a grown-up man, and I loved each and every minute!

Looking for the Dead!

One spring morning, Miss Cornelia called my father and asked if he had seen Mr. Henry Walker. They lived not too far from my house. I seemed that Mr. Henry Walker had been missing for four or five days, and Miss Cornelia had started to wonder some.

Mr. Henry kind of vanished every spring about the time I was climbing the mulberry trees. The fruit is sweet and can only be gotten for a week or so in the late spring. It never fails to come into being about the time of the first cutting of hay. For country boys, it is a wonderful time with the smell of hay and the sweet mulberries.

Mr. Henry Walker, like many of the men on the Ridge, was given to taking a drink of strong moonshine. Come spring a person's mouth and palate go to looking for something a little smoother and gentler than straight moonshine. As soon as the hay is in the barn, Appalachian men take to looking and checking on the mulberries. Once they are ripe, a gallon or two of moonshine is found. About a quart of the moonshine is either drunk or poured into a second jar. The moonshine jar is filled with fresh, sweet, pink mulberries and given a good shake. The mulberry moonshine is then set there, right up on the last bale of hay pitched into the barn, to let it absorb all of the beautiful color and grand taste. After about two weeks, the men on the Ridge just kind of vanish in the late afternoons.

Well, Mr. Henry Walker had done vanished for almost a week, and as I said, Miss Cornelia was starting to wonder some. She called Daddy and asked him to walk over to the small barn on the little hill with apple trees and look and see if Mr. Henry was dead. "He just might have fallen in the cistern or something. I know that he made a gallon or two of the mulberry moonshine he likes so much."

You think Daddy would go? Hell, no. I am only seven or eight years old, and he sends me to look for Mr. Henry. I slowly walk up through the orchard to the little barn. I come up to the cistern first and take the pole and slide the cover off. I do not see Mr. Henry floating around in there. I holler back to Daddy that I did not see him down the cistern drownt. Daddy says for me to go on to the barn and look around for him.

I walk into the small barn, and there in the dark lays Mr. Henry. He sure enough does look dead to me, but I am a-sceart to touch him, so I go out and find a long stick and poke him in the ribs. Damn if this corpse of a gray-looking man does not look straight at me and ask, "What in hell are you doing boy? You could hurt a man with a stick."

322

I run out of the barn and holler back across the ridge to Daddy: "Sure enough, he is in the barn. He says he ain't dead, but I'm not sure if I believe him or not. You ort to see him!"

He was very dirty and smelled as bad as the barn. He had on the same clothes that he had had on when he took to chasing after them jars of mulberry moonshine. Over the past few days, he had lost both tops and bottoms of his false teeth, so his face was all sunk in, too.

You ain't going to believe this, but every spring I go in search of mulberry trees. I eat a gallon or two, just enough to make me sick on my stomach for a couple of days. But I always come away with enough to make myself a gallon of good sweet, rosy-colored mulberry moonshine. I just let it set in the shade of the tree with the big rope hammock. Golly, it is smooth and satisfying. Yes, I still do the very things I watched those men on the Ridge do before me.

Charles Lytton

MY BROTHER, THE RIVER

Made in the USA
Columbia, SC
14 June 2017